Korean Mythology

Captivating Myths, Legends, and Folktales from Korea

© Copyright 2021

The contents of this book may not be reproduced, duplicated or transmitted without direct written permission from the author.

Under no circumstances will any legal responsibility or blame be held against the publisher for any reparation, damages, or monetary loss due to the information herein, either directly or indirectly.

Legal Notice:

This book is copyright protected. This is only for personal use. You cannot amend, distribute, sell, use, quote or paraphrase any part or the content within this book without the consent of the author.

Disclaimer Notice:

Please note the information contained within this document is for educational and entertainment purposes only. Every attempt has been made to provide accurate, up to date and reliable complete information. No warranties of any kind are expressed or implied. Readers acknowledge that the author is not engaging in the rendering of legal, financial, medical or professional advice. The content of this book has been derived from various sources. Please consult a licensed professional before attempting any techniques outlined in this book.

By reading this document, the reader agrees that under no circumstances is the author responsible for any losses, direct or indirect, which are incurred as a result of the use of information contained within this document, including, but not limited to, —errors, omissions, or inaccuracies.

Free Bonus from Captivating History (Available for a Limited time)

Hi History Lovers!

Now you have a chance to join our exclusive history list so you can get your first history ebook for free as well as discounts and a potential to get more history books for free! Simply visit the link below to join.

Captivatinghistory.com/ebook

Also, make sure to follow us on Facebook, Twitter and Youtube by searching for Captivating History.

Contents

INTRODUCTION 1
PART I: MYTHS OF KINGS AND HEROES 4
PART II: ANIMAL TALES 30
PART III: FAMILY TALES 53
PART IV: DRAGONS, SPIRITS, AND HEAVENLY BEINGS 74
HERE'S ANOTHER BOOK BY CAPTIVATING HISTORY THAT YOU MIGHT LIKE 93
FREE BONUS FROM CAPTIVATING HISTORY (AVAILABLE FOR A LIMITED TIME) 94
BIBLIOGRAPHY 95

Introduction

Korean mythology bears the imprint of Korean history, ranging from tales steeped in ancient native shamanistic traditions to legends of the exploits of Buddhist monks to stories that exemplify Confucian values. The earliest Korean religions—and the myths that go along with them—date at least to the foundation of the kingdom of Old Choson in the twenty-third century BCE and are still practiced by some Koreans today. Buddhism was introduced into Korea in the fourth century, where it was adopted by the kingdoms of Koguryo and Silla. Neo-Confucianism became ascendant during the reign of the Choson Dynasty, which ruled Korea between 1392 and 1910.

There is no single unified corpus of Korean mythology, not least because Korea's culture is not and has not been monolithic. The Allies created the states that are now known as North and South Korea at the end of World War II, but at the time that many of the myths retold in this volume were created—or at least at the time in which the events they relate were supposed to have happened—Korea was divided into three primary kingdoms: Koguryo in the north; Silla, which was situated on the western side of the peninsula and occupied much of central and South Korea; and Paekche, which was located on the southeastern part of the peninsula. Each of these kingdoms had its own foundation myths, histories, and responses to religious practice changes and philosophy that happened over time.

Two important repositories of Korean myths and legends are the *Samguk yusa* ("Memorabilia of the Three Kingdoms") and *Samguk sagi* ("History of the Three Kingdoms"). *Samguk yusa* contains foundation myths and many legends and folktales and was compiled in the late thirteenth century by a Korean Buddhist monk named Iryeon (1206-1289). *Samguk sagi*, by contrast, was an attempt at an official history of Korea and was compiled in the twelfth century at the behest of King Injong of Goryeo by Kim Busik, who was a court historian. Kim also had help from several assistants. (The kingdom of Goryeo combined Koguryo, Silla, and Paekche into a single kingdom in the tenth century.)

Both *Samguk yusa* and *Samguk sagi* are written in Classical Chinese rather than Korean because Chinese was the official language of state business and Korean literature in this period—much the same way as Latin was, which still remained the official language of the Roman Catholic Church. In addition to the literary tales preserved by *Samguk yusa* and *Samguk sagi*, there was and still remains a significant corpus of oral myth and legend, which began to be studied and recorded by Korean scholars in the 1930s.

This volume of Korean myths and legends is divided into four parts. The first contains tales about kings and heroes and presents the foundation myths of the kingdoms of Old Choson and Koguryo. Two other tales explain the origins of tutelary gods called upon for protection, and the final story follows the exploits of a brave archer who helps a dragon rid himself and his family of a murderous demon.

In the second section, animal tales are presented, and stories about families and familial relationships follow in the third section. Many of these stories exemplify important Korean values, such as filial piety, loyalty, kindness, and generosity.

The final section contains stories about mythical beings such as spirits, dragons, and heavenly maidens. Most of these are myths that follow fictional characters' actions, but the final story is a legend that grew up around an actual historical person, a Buddhist monk named Wongwang.

Korean mythology is full of delightful and vibrant characters, from dragons who live in palaces under the sea to the sons of divine beings who establish new kingdoms to clever rabbits and loving moles who only want a good husband for their daughter. Each of these tales has something new and fresh to offer, and each of them gives important insights into Korean culture and values.

Part I: Myths of Kings and Heroes

The Legend of Tangun

"The Legend of Tangun" is one of Korea's foundation myths. In this story, Hwanung, the son of the creator god Hwanin, decides to go to earth. Hwanung's son, Tangun, goes on to found Choson. The Old Choson kingdom was located in North Korea and extended into Manchuria in China, and was founded c. 2333 BCE. As with many other kingdoms and dynasties throughout history, the rulers of Old Choson attempted to establish their legitimacy by claiming descent from heavenly beings. Today, Koreans in both the north and south celebrate Tangun's founding of Choson every year on October 3.

There came a time when Hwanung desired to leave Heaven and go down to the earth to live among human beings.

Hwanung went to his father Hwanin and said, "Honorable father, I desire to go down to the earth and live among human beings."

"Go with my blessing," Hwanung said. "Go and live on the peak of Mount Taebaek. That is the best place for you to live."

And so it was that Hwanung descended to earth with three thousand spirits to help him. Hwanung also took the heavenly seals given to him by his father, and he began to rule over the people. Aiding him in his rule was the Earl of Wind, the Master of Rain, and the Master of Cloud. Hwanung established his abode in Sacred City, which he built on the mountain, and then set himself to order the people's lives. He supervised three hundred and sixty areas of human life, including agriculture, health and sickness, punishments for crime, and how long the people were allowed to live.

One day, a bear and a tiger came to speak to Hwanung.

"O great Hwanung," they said, "we wish to become people and live among the human beings."

"I will not grant that wish," Hwanung said. "It is good that you should be a bear and a tiger. Learn to be content with the forms you have."

After a few days, the bear and tiger again came to Hwanung and said, "O great Hwanung, we took thought about your wish that we remain bear and tiger, but our hearts are still troubled. We still wish to become people and live among the human beings."

"I already told you I would not do that for you. Leave, and go live good lives as tiger and bear," Hwanung said.

Again and again, the tiger and bear came to Hwanung and asked to be turned into people. They came so often that finally, Hwanung gave in.

"Since the only thing that will make you stop asking is to give you what you want, I shall tell you how you can become human. Here are twenty cloves of garlic and some sacred mugwort. Take them into that cave. Eat nothing but the garlic and mugwort, and stay inside the cave for one hundred days. If you follow those rules, you will turn into people."

The bear and tiger thanked Hwanung. They took the garlic and mugwort and went into the cave. They remained in the cave for twenty-one days, eating the garlic and mugwort and avoiding the sun's light. After twenty-one days, the bear turned into a woman. The tiger, however, did not receive a human body because he got tired of being in the cave eating nothing but garlic and mugwort. He left the cave before the hundred days were over and stayed a tiger for the rest of his days.

The Bear Woman left the cave and went looking for a husband, but she could not find any man who would marry her. She went to the foot of the sacred sandalwood tree and prayed.

"Oh, how I wish I had a child," she prayed, day after day after day.

Finally, one day, Hwanung saw her praying there. He saw how beautiful she was and how much she wanted a child, so Hwanung took human form and went to the woman. They lay down together, and soon the woman found herself with child. When her time came, she delivered a beautiful, strong baby boy that she called Tanung.

Soon, Tanung grew to manhood.

"Mother," he said, "I must go into the world and establish my kingdom."

"Go with my blessing, my son," Bear Woman, said and so Tanung left the sacred mountain.

Tanung established the city of Pyongyang to be the capital of his country, which he called Choson, which means "Bright Morning." After a time, Tanung moved to the city of Asadal on Mount Paegak, and there he was king for fifteen hundred years. Later he moved to Changdanggyong and then back to Asadal. When he was one thousand nine hundred and eight years old, he became a mountain god.

The Legend of King Tongmyong

This story is the foundation legend of the ancient Korean kingdom of Koguryo. Located in North Korea, Koguryo existed between the first century BCE and the seventh century CE. Koguryo fell in 668 when it was invaded by the allied armies of the Chinese T'ang dynasty and the smaller South Korean state of Silla. It is Koguryo that gives the modern country of Korea its name.

Haemosu and Yuwha

There came a time when Haemosu, a true Son of Heaven, decided to come down to earth. He mounted his chariot, which was pulled by five fierce dragons. His retinue numbered in the thousands, and musicians played and sang all the way down. Haemosu came down during the day, but he would return to his abode in the heavens at night.

Now, not far from where Haemosu stayed during the day was a great river. The Earl of the River had three beautiful daughters who liked to go and bathe in a pool called Heart of the Bear. One day, Haemosu went out hunting and happened to spy the three young women as they sported and played in the water. The beauty of the young women pierced his heart, and he desired to marry one of them. But when the young women saw a man staring at them, they dove into the water and swam back down to their father's palace at the bottom of the river.

"I will just have to wait here until they come back," Haemosu said. "But I can't just sit here on the riverbank. I need a proper palace."

So, Haemosu took his riding crop and used it to trace the foundations of a beautiful palace. Haemosu waved his riding crop, and walls appeared, followed by beautiful tiled roofs and windows with the clearest glass. Again, he waved his riding crop, and the palace was full of soft cushions and the best food and wine. When the palace was finished, Haemosu went inside to wait.

One day, the Earl of the River's daughters went to bathe in the Heart of the Bear pool. They were startled to see a beautiful palace on the banks of the river.

"Let's go and see who lives there," they said.

And so, they went to the palace, where they found the gates open. They came to a room where food and wine had been set out, and so they sat down and made a merry meal. Soon they had drunk quite a bit of wine, which made them laugh and sing.

When Haemosu heard the women singing and laughing, he went to the dining room. The women saw him and started to run away, but Haemosu caught one of them, the most beautiful of them all, and her name was Yuhwa, which means "Willow Flower."

"Don't be afraid," Haemosu said. "I love you and want you to be my wife. Please stay here with me."

Willow Flower agreed, so Haemosu sent a messenger to the Earl of the River asking for his daughter's hand.

The earl was enraged by this.

He stormed over to Haemosu's palace and said, "How dare you ask for my daughter like this! This isn't the proper way to contract a marriage at all. You should have sent your go-between to me, and then I would send mine to you, and then we'd negotiate the terms of the marriage contract. But you've just gone and stolen my daughter! This is shameful! Who do you think you are?"

"I am Haemosu, noble sir, and I am a true Son of Heaven. I love your daughter, and want her to be my wife."

"Son of Heaven, eh? Well, you'll have to prove that to me before I will believe it. Let's have a shape-changing contest. If you can best me, then I'll know you are who you say you are."

"That is fair. Let us begin."

The two men walked to the riverbank, where the earl dove into the water and changed himself into a carp. Haemosu dove in after him and turned into an otter. In no time at all, the otter had caught the carp. The earl then changed himself into a pheasant and flew up into the sky. Haemosu followed in the form of an eagle. He nearly had the pheasant in his talons when the Earl of the River turned himself into a stag and went bounding into the forest. Haemosu took the shape of a wolf and gave chase.

When the earl realized that he would never be able to beat Haemosu, he took his own form and said, "I give in. You truly are a Son of Heaven. Let us go and drink together to seal the marriage contract."

The two men went to the earl's palace, where they drank cup after cup after cup of wine. Now, Haemosu had been living among human beings during the day for some time, but he had never quite gotten used to human wine, and soon he was quite drunk. The earl put Haemosu into a leather bag and then put the bag on the dragon chariot. Then he put Yuwha onto the chariot next to the bag. As the chariot began rising through the water, Haemosu woke up and found himself inside the bag. He sliced a hole in the bag with one of Yuwha's hairpins and climbed out, but as he did so, he knocked Yuwha off the chariot and back into the water. Haemosu returned to Heaven without his wife.

The Birth of Chumong

Now, the earl had pretended to welcome Haemosu as his son-in-law, but in truth, he was still livid.

The earl went to his daughter and said, "You brazen hussy, going into a strange man's palace and letting him put his hands on you! You are no daughter of mine. Get out of my house!"

The earl put a curse on his daughter that made her lips stretch and stretch until they were three feet long. Then he banished her and her maidservants to the Ubal River. There Yuwha lived, sad and mute, for she could not speak because of the length of her lips.

One day, some fisherman sailed down the Ubal River hoping to catch some fish. There they saw Yuwha and her maidservants playing in the water. They stared at Yuwha and her long lips and wondered what manner of creature she could possibly be.

"What should we do?" one of the fishermen asked.

"I'm not sure. Maybe we should ask the king," his companion replied.

The fishermen went to the capital city and begged an audience of King Kumwa.

"O most noble king," the fishermen said. "We were on the Ubal River today and saw the most marvelous creature. It looked like a woman, but it had very long lips and played in the water like a fish. We wondered what we should do about it. You are wise, and we will follow your advice."

King Kumwa replied, "Go back to the river. Catch this creature, and bring her to me."

The fishermen went back to the river. Yuwha and her maidens were still disporting themselves in the current. The fishermen cast their net and caught Yuwha.

She was very frightened and struggled to get away, but the fishermen said, "Don't be afraid. We're not going to harm you. King Kumwa told us to come and get you and bring you to see him."

When Yuwha was brought before the king, he asked her many questions, but she could not answer because of the length of her lips. King Kumwa sent for his most learned doctors.

"See whether you can trim her lips so that she can speak," the king said.

It took the doctors three tries before they could return Yuwha's lips to their normal length.

Then Yuwha said to the king, "I am the daughter of the Earl of the River. My father exiled me and cursed my lips because I went into the house of a Son of Heaven without his knowledge or consent. The Son of Heaven is named Haemosu. He fell in love with me and wanted to marry me, but my father was opposed. Haemosu went back up into the heavens on our wedding day. I have not seen him since."

King Kumwa thought this was a very strange tale, but he felt sorry for the young woman. He gave her a comfortable room to stay in and made sure her every need was met. Whenever the sun shone into her chamber, her body glowed. If she moved from one part of the room to another, the beams of the sun followed her.

It soon became apparent that the young woman was pregnant. When her time came, she gave birth to a great egg. The king took the egg and put it in the pigsty, but the pigs would not eat it. The king then took the egg and put it in the pasture, but the cows and horses merely walked around it. He took it into a forest meadow, and the birds gathered around it and shaded it with their wings. The king became angry and tried to break the egg, but no matter how hard he hit the egg, the egg would not break, no matter how sharp the tool was.

Finally, the king took the egg back to Yuwha. Yuwha covered the egg with a fine cloth and then set it in the sunniest part of the room. After a few moments, the egg burst open. Inside the egg was a boy child, perfectly formed and more beautiful than anyone had ever seen before.

By the time the child was seven years old, he was already making his own bows and arrows. It did not matter what target he pointed his arrows at; he always made the shot. For this reason, they gave him the name Chumong, which means "Good Archer."

King Kumwa brought Chumong up with the king's own seven sons, but none of the princes was a match for Chumong. Chumong always bested them in every game and sport, and soon the princes became jealous.

When Chumong and the princes were grown to manhood, the crown prince went to King Kumwa and said, "You really should do something about that Chumong. He could be dangerous. You've seen how skilled he is. It's only a matter of time before he tries to take your throne."

King Kumwa decided to test Chumong's loyalty by putting him in charge of the royal stables. Chumong obeyed the king, but in his heart, he felt angry and ashamed.

"I am a Son of Heaven," Chumong said to himself. "I should have a position of high honor, not be given the duties of a herdsman. I should be a king in my own land."

Yuwha heard what her son said.

She went to him and said, "You are right, my son. You should leave, not least because I think the princes are plotting against you. But first, you need to choose a horse, and then you need to choose some companions to go with you."

Mother and son went to the paddock where the king's horses were kept. Yuwha took out a whip and started making the horses fearful, so they would bolt. One of them ran straight for the paddock wall and jumped right over it, even though it was taller than a man.

"That is the horse you should take," Yuwha said.

"The king will never allow it. That's the best horse in his herd," Chumong said.

"Leave that to me."

Yuwha coaxed the horse back into the paddock, where she put a small needle into its tongue so that it would not eat. After several days, the horse became thin and listless. When King Kumwa came to inspect the stables, he saw that that horse wasn't doing well.

"That horse is not fit for a king. Therefore, I give him to you. He is yours to do with as you wish," Kumwa said.

Chumong then removed the needle from the horse's tongue and fed it well.

Soon the horse was strong and fat, and its coat was glossy.

Chumong then went to his three closest friends and said, "I am leaving tomorrow. I am a Son of Heaven, and I intend to found my own kingdom. A king needs trusty companions and advisors. Will you come with me?"

The three men said they would gladly come, and when all was ready, Chumong bid a tearful farewell to his mother and rode out of the city with his friends.

Chumong Establishes His Kingdom

The four men rode toward the south until they came to the Omsa River. The river was broad and swift, but it had no bridge, and there was no ferry.

Chumong raised his hands to the sky and said, "I am the Grandson of Heaven and the Grandson of the River. Here I am with no one to help me. I must cross the river. Who will give me aid?"

Then he took his bow and struck the water with it. In just a few moments, turtles and fish rose out of the water. They linked their bodies together, and soon there was a shining bridge all the way from one side of the river to the other.

Now, when King Kumwa found out that Chumong had tricked him out of a good horse and fled the city, he was furious. He commanded the captain of the guard to take a company of picked men to find Chumong and bring him back, dead or alive. The guards caught up with Chumong and his friends just as they were crossing the bridge that the turtles and fishes had made. As soon as Chumong and his companions reached the far bank of the river, the fish and turtles let go and fell back into the water, leaving no way for the pursuing guards to cross to the other side.

Riding ever southward, Chumong and his friends soon came to a fair land with thick forests and many streams and rivers on its mountainsides.

"This is a good place," Chumong said. "I will make my kingdom here." Chumong took out his royal mat and sat upon it. "I am no longer Chumong, the Good Archer. Now I am King Tongmyong, Light of the East, and my land shall be called Koguryo."

Tongmyong established his kingdom and assured the loyalty of his subjects. In the city of Moso, he built a large house above the Piryu River to live in, and he administered the country well with the aid of his courtiers.

One day, Chumong went out hunting, and he came across another party of hunters. These people clearly were nobles, and Chumong wondered who they were and where they were from.

A man who seemed to be the leader of the group of hunters approached Chumong and said, "Greetings, I am King Songyang, and you are in my land, which is called Piryu-guk. Who are you, and where do you come from?"

"My name is Tongmyong, and I am the son of a Son of Heaven. I have established my own kingdom and rule it from my capital, Moso."

"I see. I, too, am of noble birth. All my forbears were kings, and we have ruled this land for generations upon generations. You may be of noble birth, but you have newly come to this place, and there isn't room for two kings in the same land. I think you should make yourself my vassal."

"That I'll not do. I am a king in my own right, and I bow to no man."

"Very well. Perhaps we should have a contest to see which of us is more deserving to rule both our lands. I see you have a bow and arrows. Shall we have an archery contest?" Songyang suggested this because he was a famous archer among his own people and had no knowledge of Chumong's skill.

"I accept your challenge," Chumong said.

Songyang told his servants to set up a wooden statue of a deer.

When the deer was in place, Songyang said, "Since you are the guest, you may shoot first. Distance is one hundred paces."

Chumong took his place one hundred paces away from the deer. He nocked an arrow to the string and let fly. Everyone watching let out a gasp of astonishment when the arrow embedded itself in the deer's navel.

"That was impressive shooting," Songyang said, "but it had to have been a fluke. No one is that good with a bow. Let's set up another target, a small jade bowl. You can shoot first again, but I'll wager you won't be as lucky this time."

When the bowl was in place, Chumong again bent his bow and let fly. The arrow went straight to the target, and soon the bowl was shattered into a hundred pieces.

Everyone who saw Chumong's feat was silent with awe.

Songyang glared at Chumong for a moment and then mounted his horse and rode away with his retinue, not saying a word.

Chumong, for his part, was pleased that he had won the contest but was still angry that Songyang thought of him as inferior and that he hadn't even had the courtesy to congratulate him or even to say goodbye.

Chumong continued with his hunt.

Suddenly, a white deer appeared. Chumong shot the deer but only wounded it.

He then tied the deer up and said, "White deer, I will never let you go free unless you do as I bid. Make it rain on Piryu. Make it rain so that everything floods. Make it rain so that the floods wash away everything in that land."

The deer began to cry, a sound so heart-wrenching that Heaven could not but answer the poor animal's plea. It rained on Piryu for seven days. It rained so hard that soon all the rivers rose and washed away the houses. It even flooded Songyang's palace.

Songyang cried out for help. "Make it stop! I agree that Tongmyong is indeed a Son of Heaven and my superior! Just make the rain stop!"

Tongmyong heard Songyang's cry. He took his riding crop and drew a line with it. The rain stopped, and the floodwaters receded. Tongmyong released the deer, as he had promised.

Suddenly, the sound of a thousand stonemasons hammering away filled the air.

All the people wailed with fright, but Tongmyong said, "Have no fear! Heaven is building me a palace up on the mountainside!"

No sooner had Tongmyong uttered those words than a mist lifted, and there on the mountain was the most beautiful palace anyone had ever seen. Tongmyong ruled over the land for nineteen years and then left the earth behind and returned to Heaven.

The Tale of Pihyong

In his translation of this story, James Greyson notes that it functions as a just-so story that explains how Pihyong became a household deity. Greyson observes that Pihyong's miraculous conception and birth, combined with his ability to control various spirits, made him a desirable patron for those who wished some protection from malevolent spirits.

Modern Western readers might wonder what Kildal did that was so bad that he deserved death. Greyson explains this by saying that Kildal's transforming himself into a fox reveals his bad nature since the fox was associated with evil spirits in Korean folklore.

Pihyong's supposed father, King Chinji, was an actual historical person. He reigned over Silla between 576 and 579 CE.

Once, there was a king of Silla named Chinji. He ruled for only four years, and this was a good thing. King Chinji did not rule wisely. He allowed his lands to fall into disorder, and the government was incompetent. The only thing Chinji really cared about was feeding his own appetites.

One day, Chinji heard of a beautiful woman named Tohwa-rang, which means "Peach Blossom." Chinji demanded first that his advisors find out as much as they could about the woman and then that she be brought to him. When Chinji saw Tohwa-rang, he burned with desire. Tohwa-rang was everything his advisors had described and more.

"I would like to be your husband," Chinji said. "What would you think of having a king for a husband, eh?"

Tohwa-rang replied, "It is said that it is bad fortune for a woman to have more than one husband at a time, noble sir. I already have a husband and so must decline your invitation."

"You know that I could have you killed for refusing me."

"Yes, I know that, but I don't want to marry you. I only want my own husband."

"What if your husband were dead. Would you consent to marry me then?"

"Yes, if my husband were dead, I would be free to marry you."

Chinji then let Tohwa-rang return to her home. Not long after Chinji had spoken to Tohwa-rang, the people of Silla rose up. They deposed Chinji and killed him.

Two years after Chinji's death, Tohwa-rang's husband also died. Ten days later, Tohwa-rang woke in the middle of the night with the strange feeling that she was being watched. She peered about in the darkness, and there at the foot of her bed was the ghost of King Chinji.

"Your husband is dead now, so you can marry me," Chinji said. "You haven't forgotten your promise, have you?"

Tohwa-rang said she had not.

"Well, then," Chinji's ghost said, "let's get married."

"I would like to discuss this with my parents first."

"Very well," the ghost said, and then it vanished.

Tohwa-rang went to speak to her parents the next morning. She told them everything that had passed between herself and Chinji, both when the king was alive and when he had visited her as a ghost.

"Should I marry him?" Tohwa-rang said. "It seems odd to marry a ghost, but I did promise."

"You could do worse than marrying the ghost of a king," Tohwa-rang's parents said. "It's odd, but he's still a king, for all that."

Tohwa-rang went home. That night, the ghost of King Chinji appeared to her again.

"So, what did your parents say?" he asked.

"They said that I should marry you if I wished," Tohwa-rang replied.

"Will you marry me?"

"Yes."

As soon as she said yes, a great cloud came down and covered Tohwa-rang's house so that not one window or eave was visible, and from the cloud came the scent of delicious perfume. The ghost of King Chinji spent seven days and seven nights with Tohwa-rang, and at the end of that time, it disappeared. Tohwa-rang soon found herself with child, and when her time came, she delivered a baby boy. Just at the moment that he was delivered, there was an earthquake. Tohwa-rang named her son Pihyong.

King Chinji's successor was a man named Chinp'yong. He heard what happened when Pihyong was born, so he sent messengers to Tohwa-rang to ask whether he might foster the child at his palace. Tohwa-rang gave her consent, so Pihyong was brought to the palace and raised by King Chinp'yong.

Pihyong grew up tall and strong and proved to be very intelligent. King Chinp'yong gave him many duties about the palace, which Pihyong did very well.

One day, some of the other palace administrators went to King Chinp'yong and said, "You know that boy Pihyong? The one with the odd birth story?"

"Yes," the king replied.

"Well, every night, he disappears. Nobody knows where he goes or what he does. He doesn't come back until dawn. Doesn't this seem odd?"

The king agreed that it was odd, so he ordered fifty of his soldiers to keep a close eye on Pihyong. The men watched Pihyong for several nights. Each night, Pihyong flew away from the palace and went to the west. A group of spirits gathered around him as they flew, and when they arrived at a stream on the slopes of a hill, they sang and danced together all night long. Just before daybreak, when the temple bells began to ring, Pihyong flew back to the palace, and the spirits disappeared.

The captain of the soldiers told the king what he and his men had seen.

The king then summoned Pihyong and said, "My men say that you fly out of the palace at night. They say that you go into the hills to the west, where you sing and dance all night with some spirits. Are my men telling me the truth? Do you really do that?"

"Most noble sir, it is the truth," Pihyong replied.

"Well, if you and your spirit friends have enough energy to dance and sing all night, maybe you can do some things for me too. There's a stream in Sinwon-sa that needs a bridge. Ask your spirit friends to help you build one there."

"As your majesty commands."

That night, Pihyong flew out with the spirits, but instead of having fun, they gathered materials to make a bridge. Before daybreak, a fine new bridge spanned the stream in the place the king had commanded it be built.

In the morning, the king summoned Pihyong again.

"Did you and your friends build the bridge?" the king asked.

"Yes, most noble sir, it is built."

"Excellent! Now, do you think one of your spirit friends might be able to turn himself into a human and help with some other things that need doing?"

"One of them is a spirit named Kildal. I think he would be willing to help if he knew it was the king who asked."

"Very well. Please ask him when you see him tonight."

The next morning, Pihyong went before the king and presented his friend Kildal, who had taken human form. The king made Kildal one of his administrators. Kildal did his work very well, and the king was pleased.

The head of all the administrators in Silla was a man named Imjong. Imjong was a good man and loyal to the king, but he had no son. King Chinp'yong asked Kildal if he would let Imjong adopt him as his son. Kildal said yes, and so he became the son of Imjong.

After Kildal had lived with Imjong for a time, Imjong said, "My son, I wish you to go to the Hungnyun-sa temple. I wish you to build a guardhouse near it. When the guardhouse is built, you will live in it."

Kildal built the guardhouse as Imjong had commanded and lived there for a time. But one night, Kildal turned himself into a fox and ran away into the hills. When Pihyong heard what Kildal had done, he ordered the other spirits to chase after Kildal and kill him, and this is why spirits are always afraid when they hear Pihyong's name. Someone even made up a song to sing, to keep the spirits away:

The spirit of the King of Heaven

Has a son named Pihyong.

Pihyong lives here;

All you bad spirits

Should fly away as fast as you can!

Pihyong lives here!

Ch'oyong and the Plague Demon

King Hongang was a historical ruler who reigned over the Korean kingdom of Silla from 875 to 886 CE. The events of the story retold below supposedly took place in 879. A formal dance involving costumed singers, including one dressed as Ch'oyong, was performed at court in Silla at the New Year to drive illness and plague away from the kingdom. A thirteenth-century version of the dance text incorporates the song Ch'oyong sings at the end of the tale below.

During the reign of King Hongang, the entire country was happy and prosperous. All the houses were roofed with tiles instead of thatch, there was always rain and sun in just the right amounts to make the crops grow, and the sound of music and song was always in the air.

One day, King Hongang decided to go to the waterside at Kaeunp'o. He spent a happy day there, delighting in the sunshine and the sea breeze. But in the afternoon, a strong wind began to blow, and the waves on the water were frothed into whitecaps. Great, billowing black clouds covered the horizon and blew toward the shore, and a thick fog came down and covered everything so that it was impossible to see even a few feet in any direction. King Hongang was greatly afraid.

He turned to his wise ministers who had accompanied him and said, "What is causing this storm? Can I do anything to make it stop?"

The king's astrologer replied, "I think I know what this is. It is a message from the Dragon of the Eastern Sea. He wants you to do some act that is both great and good. If you do such a thing, the Dragon will be content, and the fog and the storm will go away."

"I will appease the Dragon very well," Hongang said. "I will build a temple in his honor, right in this very spot."

Hongang sent for architects and builders, and soon a beautiful temple dedicated to the Dragon of the Eastern Sea stood near the beach. No sooner had the last nail been pounded than the fog lifted, the wind subsided to a gentle breeze, and the clouds drifted away. Everyone was in awe of the beautiful temple, which shone with gold and whose roof tiles glinted in the bright sun.

The Dragon of the Eastern Sea saw the temple that Hongang had built, and he was greatly pleased by it.

The Dragon called his seven sons and said, "We are going to pay King Hongang a visit of state. He has erected a beautiful temple for me, and we need to go and thank him."

The Dragon and his seven sons came up out of the waves. King Hongang, who was there for the dedication of the temple, bowed low.

"Welcome, Lord Dragon," King Hongang said, "and welcome to your many fine sons."

"Greetings, King Hongang," the Dragon said. "My sons and I have come to thank you for the temple you have built. Your architects and craftsmen have plied all their skill, and I am most honored."

Then the Dragon and his sons danced and sang in the king's honor.

King Hongang thanked the Dragon and his sons for their song and dance and said, "I must return to my palace now. Would any of you care to come with me and be my guest? I would be honored for you to stay in my home even for a little while."

The seventh son of the Dragon said, "Father, may I go? I would like to see King Hongang's palace and see what his country looks like."

"Certainly," the Dragon said. "You may go with King Hongang and stay as long as he will have you."

The seventh son, whose name was Ch'oyong, accompanied Hongang on the journey back to his palace. Hongang gave Ch'oyong his own apartments and saw to it that he lacked for nothing. Ch'oyong proved to be very wise, and soon he was one of Hongang's most trusted advisors. Hongang arranged for Ch'oyong to marry a beautiful woman, and so Ch'oyong lived in great contentment for a long while.

One day, the Plague Demon looked upon Ch'oyong's wife and desired her. The Plague Demon transformed himself into a handsome man, and when Ch'oyong was away, he went into Ch'oyong's wife's bedroom and seduced her. Ch'oyong came home while his wife and the Plague Demon were in bed together. Ch'oyong wasn't fooled by the Demon's disguise; he knew who was in bed with his wife. Ch'oyong began to dance and sing to drive away the Demon, and this is what Ch'oyong sang:

Tonight I went out into the city

To dance and sing with my friends.

And now I come home to find

Four legs in my bed

Where there should only be two.

I wonder who has stolen

The two legs that once were mine?

The Plague Demon heard Ch'oyong's song and became very frightened. He leaped out of Ch'oyong's bed and took his own disgusting shape.

The Demon knelt in front of Ch'oyong and said, "Yes, it is I who seduced your wife. It was an evil thing to do, and I beg your forgiveness. From now on, I will not enter the home of anyone who hangs your likeness above their door."

And this is why even today, people hang pictures of Ch'oyong's face above the doors of their homes.

Kot'aji and the God of the Western Sea

This story is set during the reign of Queen Chinsong, who lived between c. 865 and 897 CE. Because her two brothers died without issue, Chinsong was able to take the throne. However, Chinsong herself does not play much of a role in this tale, which centers on the adventures of an archer named Kot'aji.

In this tale, dragons are first encountered, one of the most important mystical beings in Far Eastern mythologies, including that of Korea. Unlike their fire-breathing western counterparts, the Far East dragons are creatures of water, and although they might cause mischief and occasionally kidnap humans and other creatures, they are largely benignant beings with the power to confer wealth and good fortune on those who treat them well.

Queen Chinsong of Silla had a son named Yangp'ae. Yangp'ae was the youngest of all of Chinsong's sons, but he was intelligent and honest, and therefore his mother trusted him greatly.

One day, Chinsong summoned Yangp'ae and said, "I need you to go on an embassy to T'ang in China. Take a good ship and as many men as you need."

Yangp'ae did as his mother asked. He commissioned a fine ship and her crew and brought along fifty of the finest archers in the land to protect the ship from the pirates who sailed the waves between Silla and China. At first, the ship had a smooth passage. The winds were in her favor, and the sea was calm. But when the ship came within sight of Kokto Island, a huge storm blew up out of nowhere. The crew reefed the sails, and the helmsman struggled with the tiller. The ship was tossed to and fro on giant waves and could make no headway but rather remained close to the island.

After several days of this, Yangp'ae consulted the advisor he had brought along to help with the embassy.

Yangp'ae said to the advisor, "You are practiced in the art of divination. See whether you can find out why this storm is keeping us here."

The advisor read the signs and said, "There is a sacred pond on this island. The deity who lives there is demanding we pay our respects. We should go and put sacrificial objects into the pond. Then we'll be able to sail away."

Yangp'ae agreed that this was a good plan and ordered that the ship sail directly for the island. The storm abated just enough for them to be able to make landfall, but it was still far too dangerous for them to sail any farther. Yangp'ae, his advisor, and the ship's captain went to the sacred pond with many precious things to offer to the deity. They threw the things into the water one by one, and when they were finished, the water in the pond suddenly heaved up and then splashed down again.

"What do we do now?" Yangp'ae asked the advisor.

"We wait and see whether the deity gives us a sign," the advisor replied.

That night, Yangp'ae had a dream in which an old man appeared to him and said, "If you leave one of your archers behind, the storm will end, and you will be able to sail on."

In the morning, Yangp'ae told his dream to all the men aboard the ship.

When he finished his tale, he said, "All of you are fine men and good archers. How shall we choose which of you is to remain behind?"

The archers discussed it among themselves for a bit and then answered, "We can cast lots. We'll each write our names on little pieces of wood. The person whose piece of wood sinks will stay behind."

The ship's carpenter took out his plane and made fifty strips of wood for the archers to use, and Yangp'ae's advisor lent them his ink and brush. When all the pieces of wood were ready, the archers all stood along the gunwales of the ship, their hands poised over the water, ready to release their pieces of wood. Yangp'ae gave the signal, and all the archers let their pieces of wood go. One of the fifty sank below the water, and this was the piece belonging to a man named Kot'aji.

"You will have to go ashore," Yangp'ae said. "We will return for you when our embassy is done, unless it becomes possible for you to leave before that."

Kot'aji bowed to his prince, bade farewell to his comrades, and then went ashore. As soon as Kot'aji's foot touched dry land, the storm completely abated, and a favorable wind blew up. The crew hoisted the sails, and the ship sailed off on the rest of its journey.

Kot'aji decided to explore the island.

"If I'm going to live here for a while," he said to himself, "I should figure out what there is to eat and drink and maybe make a shelter. This fine weather isn't going to hold forever."

In the course of his exploration, Kot'aji came across the sacred pond. As he stood gazing at the clear, still water, ripples formed on the surface of the pond. The ripples grew bigger and bigger, and soon the center of the pond was a boiling mass of bubbles. Out of the mass of bubbles rose a form that looked like it might be a person. Soon the form took the clear shape of an old man.

Kot'aji bowed to the man.

Then the man said, "I am the God of the Western Sea. I'm the one who asked for an archer to stay behind. I saw your ship coming my way, with so many fine archers aboard, and I just couldn't miss that chance. Thank you for staying on my island."

"You are most welcome, honorable one. What can I do for you?"

"My family is in terrible distress. Every day, a creature that looks like a monk comes to the pond and summons me and my family. It chooses one of my children, kills them, and eats their liver. The creature has eaten all but one of my children, my dearest daughter. Can you wait near the pond in the morning and use your bow to kill that creature?"

Kot'aji felt sorry for the god and his family. He said, "I surely will help you, honorable one. It shall be as you ask, and soon your family will be free."

In the morning, Kot'aji concealed himself in the trees near the pond and waited for the monk-creature to arrive. Not long after daybreak, a figure floated down from the sky. It took the shape of a monk and began to walk around the pond while chanting strange words. Kot'aji put an arrow to the string and let fly. The arrow hit the creature right in the heart. It cried out once in pain and then transformed into the shape of a fox and died.

As before, the pond waters began to roil, and the old man appeared. He saw the dead fox with Kot'aji's arrow sticking out of its side.

"Oh, thank you, thank you!" the old man said. "You have delivered me and my family. I would like to do something good for you in return. Will you take my daughter's hand in marriage?"

"I will be honored to be your daughter's husband," Kot'aji said, "and I will do my best to be good to her for all my days."

The waters of the pond roiled again, and soon a lovely young woman was standing next to the old man.

"This is my daughter," the old man said. "She has agreed to be your wife."

The young people gazed upon one another and instantly fell in love.

"Now, we have to get you off this island," the old man said. "This is no place for a young couple to start a family."

The old man and his daughter said their farewells. Then the old man transformed his daughter into a flower and gave it to Kot'aji.

"Keep this flower safe, for it is my daughter and your wife. She will turn back into a woman when you arrive safely on dry land," the old man said.

Kot'aji promised to look after the flower and placed it inside his shirt next to his heart.

"Now, to return you to your prince," the old man said. "Come with me to the beach. I'll provide you with a ship."

Kot'aji and the old man went to the beach. A small but sturdy ship appeared. Kot'aji said farewell to the old man and boarded the ship.

"Thank you for the ship," Kot'aji said, "but I'm an archer, not a sailor. I don't know how to steer or sail."

"Never fear. Two of my friends will help you."

At that, two dragons appeared: one at the prow and the other at the stern. The dragons propelled the little ship faster than the wind until they neared Yangp'ae's ship, which was still about half a day out from T'ang. Yangp'ae and the others aboard the ship were pleased to see Kot'aji and very impressed indeed by the manner of his arrival. Kot'aji stayed in the dragon ship until they arrived on the coast of T'ang. Envoys who had been sent to keep watch for the embassy from Silla saw Yangp'ae's fine ship and Kot'aji's dragon ship and ran to tell the emperor who was arriving.

"We must make the embassy from Silla as welcome as we can," the emperor said. "Anyone who merits a dragon ship as part of their flotilla must be treated with the highest respect."

The emperor commanded that a fine banquet be prepared and invited Yangp'ae, Kot'aji, and all the crew and archers to attend. The finest food and drink were served, and the emperor gave many costly gifts to the men from Silla. Yangp'ae and the emperor had several fruitful talks together, and soon it was time for the men from Silla to return home. Kot'aji kept the flower next to his heart all the way home. When he disembarked, he took it out, and it turned into a woman. Kot'aji and the sea god's daughter had a joyful wedding provided by Queen Chinsong herself, and Kot'aji and his wife lived together in much happiness until the end of their days.

Part II: Animal Tales

The Mole and the Mireuk

This simple folktale centers around the universal desire of parents to marry their children well. In this case, a family of moles wants to make the best marriage possible for their daughter.

This tale's mireuk *is probably a Buddhist stone carving representing the Maitreya, a figure who Buddhists believe will return in the far future to lead humanity to a just and peaceful existence. However, the mireuk also exists in Korean folklore as a god of fertility and is often represented by a standing stone carved into a phallic shape.*

There once was a family of moles who lived in cozy little tunnels under the ground. They lived near a statue of a mireuk, which stood just outside a temple. The mother mole and father mole were very handsome, with shining, soft fur, but neither could compare with their daughter. She was the most beautiful mole anyone had ever seen.

One day, the father mole went to the mother mole and said, "It is high time our daughter got married, Mother."

"Yes, Father," the mother mole said. "I agree that she is ready for a husband. Who shall we ask to marry our daughter?"

"Our daughter is the most beautiful and most precious thing in the whole world, so we must marry her to the most powerful person we can find. No one must be more powerful than our daughter's husband."

"What about the king of the moles? He is very powerful indeed."

"Yes, but he is not the most powerful. I think we should ask the sky. The sky looks down on everyone, even the king of the moles."

And so, the father mole set out to ask the sky to marry his daughter. It took him a long time, but finally, he arrived at the sky's home.

"O sky," the father mole said, "I am looking for a husband for my daughter. I respectfully ask you to marry her because you are the most powerful being in the whole world."

"I am honored to be asked," the sky said, "but I am not the most powerful. The sun is more powerful than I am because he tells me whether I can be the blue of the day or the black of the night or any of the colors in between."

So, the father mole resumed his journey.

He went all the way to the house of the sun, and when he arrived, he said, "O sun, I am looking for a husband for my daughter. Would you consent to marry her? I am asking because you are the most powerful being in the world, and only the most powerful being is good enough for my daughter."

"Thank you for asking me," the sun said, "but I am not the most powerful. You should go and talk to the king of the clouds. The cloud is the one who decides whether my light goes all the way to the earth or not. If he stands in my way, there is nothing I can do about it! Go talk to the king of the clouds."

The father mole journeyed on and on. Finally, he came to the home of the king of the clouds.

"O king of the clouds," the father mole said, "I am looking for a husband for my daughter. I have been told that you are the most powerful being in the whole world. Will you consent to marry my child?"

"You honor me," the king of the clouds said. "But although I am very powerful, I am not the most powerful. The wind is more powerful than I. One puff of his breath can blow me quite away!"

The father mole then set out to find the wind. He searched up and down and all around, and finally, he found the wind's home.

"O wind," the father mole said, "I understand that you are the most powerful being in the whole world. I would like you to marry my daughter because she deserves such a powerful husband as you."

"I'm sure your daughter is a very fine young mole," the wind said, "but I am not the most powerful being. That title belongs to the mireuk who stands near your own home. I can't tell you how many times I have tried to blow that mireuk down, but he just stands there like nothing is happening!"

The father mole turned and headed for home.

"I hope the mireuk consents to marry our daughter," he said. "I am tired of journeying up and down and all around. I want to find our daughter a nice husband so that she will be happy and safe and so that I can stop traveling all over the world."

Finally, the father mole arrived at the temple.

He stood at the feet of the mireuk and said, "O mireuk, I am looking for a husband for my daughter. I have been told that you are the most powerful being in the whole world. Would you consent to be my daughter's husband?"

"It is very kind of you to ask me," the mireuk said. "And it is true that I am very powerful. The sky looks down on me, the sun beats down on me, the clouds rain and snow on me, and the wind tries to blow me down, but still, I stand strong and tall. But I am not the most powerful. There is one creature on earth more powerful than I am, and I'm afraid of it."

"What creature is that?" the father mole asked.

"It is the mole. If a mole should ever tunnel under my feet, I shall fall right over and shatter into a dozen pieces, and that would be the end of me! No, if you want your daughter to marry someone powerful, you should find a nice mole husband for her. Then she will be very happy."

And so, it was that the mother and father moles found a very nice mole husband for their beautiful daughter. The young couple was very happy together, and the mole parents were all glad they had made such an advantageous match for their children.

Why Cats and Dogs Are Enemies

This just-so story explains the origins of the enmity between cats and dogs, which arises when the cat fails to keep its mind on its mission. The story centers around the search for a piece of magical amber, which the dog and the cat identify by its scent. Natural amber is a fossilized form of resin produced by certain coniferous trees. As such, it retains a faint scent that tells of its origins.

There is also another old Korean tradition in this story, which is carrying money on a string. In the past, Korean coins were pierced; threading them on strings made for easy carrying and storage.

Once there was an old man who had a wine shop on the banks of a river near a ferry landing. Although he only ever sold one kind of wine, and only sold it to people who brought their own vessels to be filled and then brought home again, the old man had a steady stream of customers because the wine was good and the shop was a respectable place, not a noisy tavern full of carousers and drunkards. Now, the truly odd thing was not that the old man only sold one kind of wine, or that his shop was respectable; no, the odd thing was that he only ever poured out the wine from a single jug, and that jug always seemed to be full. The old man clearly did not make his own wine, and no one ever saw barrels being unloaded from carts and then wheeled into the shop. But since the wine was good and the old man was a good neighbor, nobody complained, and nobody asked questions.

The old man was unmarried and had no children, but he did not live alone. With him lived a little dog with a curly tail and a rough coat, and a striped cat. The dog and the cat got along famously because this was in the time before dogs and cats learned to hate each other, and you will soon learn how that came about.

The old man had not always kept a wine shop. In his younger days, he was the ferryman, and made his living taking people from one side of the river to the other. One night, he moored his ferry and walked his weary way home. It had been a cold and stormy day, and he was glad to be done with his work and was looking forward to a hot meal next to a warm fire. Barely had the old man changed into dry clothing and prepared his meal when there came a knock on the door. The old man opened the door and saw a poorly dressed traveler, soaked to the skin and shivering.

"The ferry's closed," the old man said. "I don't take anyone in the dark."

"I don't need the ferry," the stranger said. "But I'm wet and very cold, and was wondering whether I might warm myself by your fire and maybe have a bite to eat and something to drink."

The traveler looked very bedraggled, so the old man felt pity for him.

"Come in," he said. "I don't have much, but you're welcome to share what I have."

The old man gave the stranger a blanket to wrap himself in then wrung out the stranger's sodden clothing and hung it over the hearth to dry. Then he gave the stranger a bowl of rice with a bit of spicy fish and some kimchee, and a cup of good wine.

"I'm afraid that's the last of the wine," the old man said, "but you seem to need it more than I do, so please do drink it all. I can get more another time."

When the meal was done and the stranger's clothing more or less dry, the stranger dressed and made ready to leave.

"Thank you for your hospitality, honorable sir," the stranger said. "I'll never forget your kindness, and I'd like to give you a gift to remember me by." The stranger handed the old man a little piece of amber. "Drop this into your wine jug, and you'll never run out of wine again."

Then the stranger went out the door and disappeared into the night.

"Well, either that was someone who is a little touched in the head, or else it was a good spirit come to test my compassion," the old man said to his dog and cat. "Either way, I'm glad I could help, even if this piece of amber is nothing more than a pretty stone."

The dog wagged his tail, and the cat purred in reply.

"What's that?" the old man asked his pets. "You want me to try it? Very well."

The old man put the wine jug on the table and dropped the amber down inside it. The amber made a loud *clink* when it hit the bottom, just as one would expect it to do in an empty jug.

"See?" the old man said. "Nothing but a pretty stone."

Then the old man lifted the jug, and to his surprise, it was as heavy as it would be if it were full, and he could hear the sound of liquid sloshing around inside it.

"Oh my!" the man exclaimed. "I guess it worked after all. Let's see what manner of wine this is."

The man poured himself a cup of the wine and took a sip. His eyes grew very wide. Then he took another sip, and another.

"This is the best wine I have ever tasted!" he said. "Blessings on that traveler who brought the stone to me!"

The man had another cup of wine to celebrate. Then he sat down and began to think.

"What do I do with this bottle, now that I have it? If I leave it here in the house, someone might take it while I'm running the ferry, but being a ferryman is the only thing I know how to do."

The man thought and thought, and then he had an idea. "I know! I'll open a wine shop. I'll make lots of money because I'll never need to make or buy any wine. The magic piece of amber that traveler gave me will do all that work for free!"

And so it was that the man opened a wine shop on the banks of the river, and another took his place as the ferryman.

The former ferryman opened his wine shop, and once word got around that good wine was to be had at a good price, he began to do a lot of business. The old man never became rich, but he was more comfortable now than when he had worked the ferry, and selling wine was a lot less strenuous.

The dog and the cat prospered, too, because their human friend could now afford a warmer, drier house and better food for all three of them.

For many years, the wine selling went along without any problems. But one day that all changed when a customer came to get their usual jug of wine. The old man took his magic jug and went to pour out a measure of wine, but the magic jug was empty! He shook the jug, but not a sound came from inside, neither the slosh of wine nor the clink of amber.

"Oh dear," the old man said to his customer. "I'm afraid that I'm fresh out and won't be getting more for a while. I'm very sorry. I'll give you a discount in compensation for having to wait when next you come back."

Now, the old man had spoken in a very calm and businesslike manner to his customer, but internally, he was shaking with anxiety. Without the piece of amber, he had no livelihood. He actually knew nothing about wine, and had no idea how to order some to sell.

"Oh dear, oh dear, oh dear!" the man said. "Whatever shall I do without that piece of amber? I must have poured it out into some other customer's jug, and I have no idea at all how to get it back. I don't even know which customer's jug it went into!"

That night, the old man went to bed very disconsolate.

However, the dog and the cat lay next to the fire and discussed what they might do to help their friend.

"Have you ever smelled amber?" the dog asked the cat.

"Yes, I smelled it once," the cat replied.

"Could you find the old man's own stone if you could smell it?"

"Yes, probably. Could you?"

"Yes, I think I could."

"That settles it, then. Tomorrow, we will work our way through the village, and even through the whole district if necessary, until we find that bit of amber. We can ask all the other dogs and cats to help us."

The dog agreed that this was a fine plan; they would start first thing in the morning.

When the sun came up, the dog and the cat set out on their mission. The dog made inquiries of the other neighborhood animals, while the cat, who was silent and stealthy, crept her way into the houses and made a thorough search. This went on for many days, and then many weeks, without any result, and soon they had searched all the houses they could find on that side of the river, and had asked all the animals who lived there too.

"We need to check on the other side of the river," the dog said.

"Yes, I agree," the cat said. "But how do we cross? We can't take the ferry. The new ferryman doesn't allow pets."

"I think we'll just have to wait until winter, when the river freezes. Then we can walk across as soon as the ice is thick enough."

"Very well."

The dog and the cat put off their search until one winter day it became clear that the river was frozen indeed. They trotted across the ice and began to search the houses on the other side of the river, and to ask the animals who lived there. The dog and the cat did this every day for several weeks, until the winter was almost over and the ice was beginning to thaw.

"We still haven't found the amber, and the ice will be melting soon," the dog said. "We really need to find the amber today."

"Yes," the cat said. "Otherwise, we'll have to wait until next winter, and who knows what might happen to the amber between now and then?"

The dog and the cat made their trek across the ice and redoubled their efforts to find the amber.

They had just reached the very last house in the late afternoon, when finally, the cat said, "Hey! Do you smell that?"

"Oh, yes!" the dog replied. "That's the amber! It's coming from in there. You can sneak in without being seen or heard, but I can't. Go see where it is. I'll wait for you here."

The cat slipped silently into the house, while the dog waited patiently in the street outside. Soon enough, the cat came back.

"Well?" the dog asked.

"I found it!"

"Where is it?"

"It's in a big wooden chest, but I don't know how to open it."

"We need help. Maybe some local rats can gnaw a hole in the chest that's big enough to get the amber out. We'll tell them that we promise to leave them alone if they help."

The dog and the cat then found some friendly rats who were willing to help. The rats went into the house and began nibbling at a corner of the chest. Soon they had a fine hole that was big enough for the amber to fit through, but not so big that the people of the house would be likely to notice it without looking for it. The cat went and put her paw in through the hole, but she couldn't reach the amber.

"We need another helper," the cat said.

"We know a mouse who's small enough," one of the rats said. "She'll help if you promise to leave the mice alone too."

The dog and the cat agreed to this plan. Presently, the mouse arrived. She slipped through the hole, found the bit of amber, and then carried it out to where the cat was waiting.

"Oh, thank you!" the cat said. "Our friend will be so pleased."

"You won't forget your promise, now, will you?" one of the rats asked.

"Certainly not. I am a cat of my word, and my dog friend is honest as well."

The cat and the dog took the amber to the riverbank, but what should they find but that the warmth of the spring day had caused the ice to begin to break up and the river to flow. It wasn't flowing as swiftly as it did in the summer or autumn, but still, there was no way to get across without swimming.

"Oh, no!" the cat cried. "How will we get home? You can't swim with the amber in your mouth, and I can't swim at all!"

"Let's do it this way," the dog said. "You carry the amber, and ride on my back. I'll do the swimming, and you do the carrying. Mind you, don't drop that stone!"

The cat accordingly took the bit of amber in its teeth and climbed up onto the dog's back, where it clung to the dog's thick fur. The dog swam across the river as fast as it could, not least because the water was very cold, but mostly because he wanted to see how happy the old man would be to have his piece of amber back. The dog and the cat had almost reached the riverbank when a group of children saw the two animals and began to laugh.

"Look!" they shouted. "It's a cat riding a dog! Have you ever seen anything so funny?"

The dog paid the children no mind; he was too busy swimming. But the cat heard their laughter, and he realized the children were right; a cat riding a dog across a river must look ridiculous indeed. The cat began to laugh along with the children, but when he opened his mouth, the bit of amber fell out and went down to the bottom of the river.

When the dog saw what had happened, he was furious. He threw the cat off his back and chased it out of the water, onto the riverbank, and up into a tree, where the cat arched its back and hissed while the dog ran in circles around the tree trunk, barking madly.

"You . . . you . . . you . . . you horrible cat!" the dog barked. "How . . . how . . . how dare you drop that piece amber! After all our hard work!"

The cat remained in the tree until the dog finally went home, and when night fell, the cat ran away and never came back. And this is why cats and dogs are now enemies; why dogs chase cats and cats hiss and spit at dogs.

But the tale does not end there. The old man did get his bit of magic amber back, and all because of his faithful dog's efforts. The dog tried many times to dive down to the riverbed to get the amber, but he could never find it.

I need to find a different way to get the amber, the dog thought. *But I don't know how.*

The dog sat on the riverbank, watching the fishermen casting their lines and pulling shining, flopping fish out of the water. This gave the dog an idea.

Maybe the amber was eaten by a fish. If I just go sniff the fish, I'll be able to smell the amber. Then I'll snatch that one fish and bring it home. Nobody will question a dog taking a sniff around fish. We do it all the time.

The dog then spent all his time trotting up and down the riverbank, poking his nose into the fishermen's creels. After many days, he finally caught the scent of amber in a fine silver fish that one of the fishermen had just landed. While the fisherman was busy with his next catch, the dog snatched up the fish and brought it home.

"It wasn't very nice to steal someone else's fish," the old man said to the dog, when the dog presented the fish. "But I don't suppose you can bring it back, and you're not going to tell me whose it is, so I guess we'll have fish for dinner tonight."

The old man slit open the fish to gut it, when what should fall out of the fish's stomach but the piece of magic amber! The old man danced and shouted with glee, and the dog barked with joy to see his master so happy.

"Oh, this is marvelous!" the old man said. "What a good dog you are! You found my magic amber! This calls for a celebration. I'm going to put on my best clothes and go buy some wine to go with dinner. You wait here. I'll be back soon."

The old man went to the chest where he kept his money and his best clothes. He changed into his best suit and took a string of money from the chest. Then he put the piece of amber into the chest and closed the lid. The old man went to a nearby wine shop and bought a jug of the best wine they had. When he got home, he opened the chest to put back the leftover money and put away his fine clothes, only to find an identical suit of clothes and another money string with the same amount he had taken out earlier!

"Oh, my!" the old man said to his dog. "I guess the amber works on clothes and money, too, not just on wine! We are going to be very rich indeed!"

And so it was that the old man became quite wealthy and lived a very comfortable life. The dog for his part kept his word and never chased another mouse or rat to the end of his days, but any cats who crossed his path were very unlucky indeed.

The Frog Husband

Many cultures have folktales centered around a handsome prince who has been turned into some kind of loathsome creature and can only be made human again by marrying a woman. Korean culture is no exception to this tradition. In Western iterations of this trope, often it is the princess who finds the frog prince and brings him home, but in this Korean tale, the frog has his adoptive family find the princess for him, and, of course, everyone lives happily ever after.

Once there was a poor farmer who lived in the mountains with his wife. The farmer worked very hard, but his land was steep and full of stones, making it difficult to grow enough food for him and his wife to eat. The wife worked very hard keeping their house and sewing their garments, but even with all her skill she could not turn poor cloth into fine silk. Even then, those were not the most sorrowful things about their lives. Although they had been married for a long time, they had never had a child, which made them very sad.

Sometimes the farmer would go to a lake near his home to catch fish. Some of them he took home for his wife and himself to eat, but most of them he brought to the village down in the valley to sell or to trade for things that he and his wife needed. He was never going to grow rich from these fish, but he always caught enough that he could make a little money and keep himself and his wife clad and fed.

One day, the farmer went to the lake to catch fish. He was concerned to see that the water level had gone down, and that some fish lay dead in the mud that ringed the lake.

I wonder what's causing that, the farmer thought. *Maybe it's because we haven't had enough rain.*

The farmer cast his line and caught some fish, but he caught many fewer than he used to.

"I'll sell all of these and come back another time. Maybe after some rain the lake will be full again."

The next time the farmer went to the lake, he saw that the water level had dropped even farther, and that there were even more dead fish lying about.

"This can't be!" he said. "We've had plenty of rain since the last time I went fishing. Oh, I hope this lake won't dry up altogether. My wife and I depend on it!"

The farmer cast his line and caught a few fish, but they were small, and there weren't enough of them to bother with the trek down the mountainside to sell them in the village.

"I'll take these home so my wife can make us a meal. That at least will be one good thing that has happened today."

A few days later, the farmer went down to the lake to go fishing again. Disaster! The lake was nearly empty of water, and dead fish were everywhere. And in the middle of the lake sat a giant frog. As the farmer watched, the frog sucked up the last of the water.

The farmer couldn't bear it.

"You!" he shouted at the frog. "Yes, you there! How dare you dry up my lake and kill all my fish! What are my wife and I to do now, you horrible old toad? How shall I water my fields? How shall I get fish to sell in the village? A curse on you and on all your relations, and on their relations too!"

"I understand why you are upset," the frog said, "and even why you called me a toad when I am, in fact, a frog. I am upset too. Now that the water is gone, I have no home. Take me home with you. Let me live with you and your wife. You won't regret it."

The farmer was nearly speechless with rage.

"I'll never take you home with me!" he shouted. "You have made my life so much harder. You have made my wife's life so much harder. No, you'll just have to hope it rains. A lot. Stay here and wait for the rain."

Then the farmer turned his back and stomped away from the frog, muttering curses under his breath the whole time.

The farmer hadn't been home for more than a few minutes when someone knocked at the door. The farmer's wife opened the door, and who should be sitting there but the giant frog.

"Please let me live with you," the frog said, its eyes glistening with tears. "I have no home. Let me live here, and good fortune will follow."

Seeing the frog's distress, the farmer relented. The farmer's wife made up a nest of damp leaves for the frog to sit in, and every so often, she poured water over the creature's green skin. At the end of the day, the wife cooked rice and vegetables and other good things for herself and her husband, and the farmer brought in a big pile of fat worms for the frog to eat. Everyone went to bed comfortable and well fed.

Early in the morning, the farmer and his wife were awakened by a loud croaking that sounded almost like a song.

"Whatever is making that racket?" the farmer asked.

"I have no idea," his wife replied. "But it sounds a lot like a frog that's trying to sing."

The farmer and his wife jumped out of bed and ran to the front of the house. The frog was not in the bed made for him, and the front door was wide open. The strange, croaking song came from just outside the door, so the farmer and his wife ran outside. There they saw the giant frog, its head pointed toward the sky, croaking out its strange tune. But this wasn't the most surprising thing they saw: no, what was even more shocking was the collection of things and people lined up in front of their house. There were huge sacks of rice and enormous jars of kimchee and baskets piled high with fruits and vegetables. There were bolts of brightly colored cloth and piles of hats and shoes. There were carpenters and painters and roofers and all manner of workmen.

As the farmer and his wife stared, the carpenters and roofers got to work, and soon the couple's modest cottage had been rebuilt into a fine home. When everything was built, the workmen brought in much fine furniture, and put away all the other goods that had stood on the front lawn. Then the workmen all bowed to the farmer and his wife, and went away down the mountainside.

"Well," the farmer said, "I guess the frog really did bring us good fortune. I take back all the bad things I said about him when I was angry."

The couple then went and bowed to the frog and thanked him profusely.

"It is no trouble," the frog said. "I am happy to help the people who help me."

The couple lived in comfort and ease for a time, and all their neighbors remarked on the strange turn in their fortune. The farmer and his wife continued to care for the frog, seeing that he lacked for nothing, for they were most grateful for all he had done for them.

Everything went very well, until one day, the frog approached the couple and said, "You have cared for me very well, but there are two other things I need you to do for me."

"Certainly," the farmer and his wife said. "You have but to name it."

The frog said to the wife, "I need you to make me a fine suit of clothes."

"Hmm," the wife said. "I'm not exactly sure how to go about sewing for a frog, but I will try. We certainly have enough good silk to clothe you well."

Then the frog turned to the farmer and said, "I need you to help me get a wife. Only the most exalted woman in the land will do. You must be my go-between, and get the hand of the woman and make the marriage contract on my behalf."

"Now wait a minute," the farmer said. "You're asking me to go to a powerful family and get them to marry their daughter to a frog? Are you out of your mind? Making a suit of clothes is one thing, but marriage to a noblewoman is quite another."

"Have I not done all that I promised, and more? Do as I ask, and your good fortune will only increase."

"Very well, but don't blame me if I'm not successful."

The farmer dressed in his very best clothes and went to pay a visit to the nobleman who lived on the other side of the village. The nobleman was aware of the change in the farmer's fortunes, and so let him into the house as an honored guest.

Now, the nobleman had three lovely daughters. Two of them were already married, and the youngest had only just come of age. This youngest daughter was very beautiful, and had been sought out by many of the other wealthy families in the neighborhood to be a wife for their sons, but her father never said yes to any of them. The farmer knew this, and was trembling with fear at what the nobleman might do when he heard why the farmer was there.

After greetings and pleasantries were exchanged, the nobleman said, "So, honorable farmer, why are you here today?"

"Most honorable sir, I am here to ask the hand of your daughter in marriage," the farmer replied.

"Indeed. Which family do you represent?"

The farmer swallowed hard. "My own, most honorable sir."

"Your own? But I know well that you and your wife are childless. Have you adopted recently?"

"You could say that, most honorable sir."

"What is this son of yours like?" the nobleman, asked his suspicions beginning to rise, for like everyone else in the district, he knew all about the frog.

"He is very polite and well bred, and he will be a most auspicious match for your lovely daughter."

"What color is his skin? What color is his hair? Is he as pale as ivory, with shining black hair, as befits a nobleman's son?"

The farmer paused, wondering whether it would be better to be truthful or excuse himself without completing his errand.

Finally, he said, "I'm afraid not, most honorable sir. He has no hair at all, and his skin is quite green."

"You want my daughter to marry that great frog of yours?" the nobleman shouted. "I have never been so insulted. I will have you beaten for this!"

The nobleman ordered his servants to tie up the farmer and beat him with paddles, but before they could strike the first blow, a great storm began, with thunder and lightning and lashing rain. The nobleman was very frightened by this, and ordered his servants to stop. No sooner had the servants untied the farmer when the storm disappeared and the sun shone brightly in a blue sky.

"It is surely an omen," the nobleman said. "I give my consent. My daughter can marry that frog of yours. But woe betide him, and you, if he mistreats her!"

When the wedding day came, the ceremony was held with great pomp. The nobleman's daughter had no idea that she was marrying a frog, for her father had told her only that he had found a worthy husband, and on the wedding day, the young woman was heavily veiled and her eyes were sealed with wax, as was the custom at the time.

After the wedding feast, the young couple were led to their chamber, where the bride took off her veil and unsealed her eyes. When she saw her frog bridegroom, she screamed and tried to run from the room, but the great frog took one leap and barred the door.

"I will never be the wife of a frog!" the young woman cried. "Oh, how I have been betrayed!"

"Most honorable wife," the frog said with great gentleness, "you will not be the wife of a frog, that I promise you most solemnly. Please trust me, as a wife ought to do, and do as I say, as a wife also ought to do."

"What do you want from me?"

"Get the knife from that bureau over there, and use it to cut open my jacket. Slit it up the back."

The young woman got the knife and cut open the jacket as she was instructed. When the pieces of the jacket fell away, the frog's green, slimy skin was exposed. It was all the young woman could do not to recoil in horror.

"What am I to do next?" the bride asked.

"Take the knife and cut open my skin. Slit it up the back, as you did with the jacket."

Very reluctantly, the young woman took the sharp knife and drew it up the frog's back along his spine. But as the skin began to split and pull apart, instead of a frog's bones and muscle was revealed the back and shoulders of a young man. When the bride stopped cutting, the frog's skin fell away, and who should stand before her but the most handsome young man she had ever seen. His skin was as pale as ivory, and his long black hair fell like a waterfall over his shoulders.

"You see? You have not married a frog at all, but a prince. My father is the King of the Stars. I did something to displease him, so he turned me into a frog, and made it so that I could not regain my true form unless I did three things. First I had to drink up all the water in a lake. Then I had to find a family to take me in and treat me as one of their own. Then I had to marry the noblest woman in the land. Thanks to the kind farmer and his wife, and to your father and yourself, I have done all those things. Now, if you consent, we will go up to my father's kingdom and live in the heavens."

The bride gladly consented, for she had fallen in love with the handsome young prince. A chariot drawn by dragons came down from the skies and took the young couple up into the heavens. And from that day forward, two new stars shone in the night sky.

The Rabbit and the Dragon King

In Korea, as elsewhere, the rabbit is a clever trickster who uses his wiles to escape all manner of predicaments. Here, the rabbit's quick wit saves him from becoming medicine for an ailing dragon.

There came a time when the Dragon King fell ill. He lay on his bed in his palace at the bottom of the sea, so weak that he could barely stand. He sent for all the wisest doctors in the world. All of them examined the Dragon King. They poked and prodded him, they looked at his scaly skin, they examined his teeth and claws, but none of them could name the malady, nor could they propose a cure. The Dragon King was becoming desperate.

"Surely I will die if a cure is not found soon," he said. "Maybe there's one more doctor who hasn't been here yet and who knows what to do."

The Dragon King sent his servants to find any doctors who had not yet visited the Dragon. Finally, they found one very old, very wise doctor and brought him down to the king's palace.

The doctor examined the Dragon King very carefully and then said, "Your malady does have a cure. You must eat a rabbit's liver."

The Dragon King then summoned the sea creatures to his palace. He asked them one by one whether they could go to find a rabbit's liver for him, but one by one, they said they could not.

Finally, only the turtle was left.

"Can you go and get a rabbit for me?" the Dragon King asked the turtle.

"Yes, I can, honorable one" the turtle replied, "but you'll need to tell me where to look. And I'll need a description of a rabbit, or a picture of one. I've never seen a rabbit before, and I don't want to bring back the wrong thing."

The Dragon King had one of the artists who lived in his palace draw a picture of a rabbit for the turtle. The artist also told the turtle where he might find such a creature.

The turtle studied the picture carefully and then said, "I know what I need to find now, honorable Lord Dragon. I'll be back as soon as I can."

The turtle swam up to the surface of the waves and then paddled his way to shore. He walked over the sand and onto the green grass that grew above the beach. It didn't take long before he spotted a rabbit nibbling at the fresh green grass. The turtle studied the rabbit for a moment to make sure he had the right creature and to devise a way to get the rabbit to come with him.

When the turtle had decided what to do, he said, "Good morning, honorable rabbit. I am an emissary from the Dragon King. His majesty the king has sent me to invite you specially to come to a feast at his palace."

The rabbit looked at the turtle with suspicion. "Why would the Dragon King want to invite me, of all creatures? Surely a creature that lives in the sea would be a better guest."

"Oh, no. His majesty asked for you specifically. He thought that you might like to see his palace. It's all carved of precious stones, and the walls are covered with silk hangings. The musicians are the best you've ever heard, and the food—it's like nothing you've ever tasted or will ever taste again! Please do come. The Dragon King so wants you to be his guest."

The rabbit was impressed by the turtle's description of the palace. "Yes, I will come. But how will I get there? The Dragon King lives at the bottom of the sea, and I can't swim very well."

"Never fear. You can ride on my back. I'll get you there safely."

The rabbit climbed up onto the turtle's hard shell, and the turtle carried him down to the sea dragon's palace. The rabbit was most impressed by the palace's beauty.

"You were right about how lovely this palace is, turtle," he said. "I can't wait to see what the feast will be like."

The rabbit went into the palace, but no sooner had he crossed the threshold than the king's guards laid hold of him and carried him to the Dragon King's chamber.

When the rabbit was stood trembling in front of the king, the king said, "Welcome to my palace, little rabbit. You are most honored today, for it is your liver that will cure me of my disease. You will always be remembered for your service. We'll hold a banquet in your memory every year on this very day."

The rabbit realized that his predicament was even worse than he had thought it was when the guards seized him. He needed to find a way out as soon as possible.

Then he had an idea.

"Noble Lord Dragon," the rabbit said, "I am flattered that you would honor me this way, but I am ashamed to admit that I came here without my liver. You see, we rabbits have to launder our livers once a month, and today was the day I did mine. I left it drying on a bush near the river. May I go and fetch it for you?"

"Certainly," the Dragon King said, "but don't be too long."

The rabbit bowed low to the Dragon King. Then he got back on the turtle's back, and the turtle brought him up to the beach. No sooner was the sand within leaping distance than the rabbit jumped off the turtle's back and ran as fast as he could up the beach and onto the grass.

"Mind you don't forget your liver," the turtle said. "I'll be waiting for you."

"You'll be waiting an awfully long time, then," the rabbit replied. "Don't you know that animals can't really take out their livers and wash them?"

Then the rabbit ran away as fast as he could, and never again did he go to the beach to nibble the sweet grass that grew above the sand.

Part III: Family Tales

Kongjwi

The common trope of an abused young woman briefly encountering a well-off young man who then seeks out the woman because he wants to marry her occurs in many cultures' folklores. Westerners know this story as "Cinderella," but in Korea, the Cinderella character is named Kongjwi, and she exhibits all the qualities one might expect in this instance. Kongjwi is kind, patient, generous, and hardworking and endures much abuse with equanimity. Just as in the Western version of the tale, Kongjwi's nasty, selfish stepmother and stepsister get their comeuppance for their mistreatment of Kongjwi and attempts to lie their ways into a marriage with the powerful government official who is looking for Kongjwi so that he can give her back her slipper.

A long time ago, a government official and his wife lived very happily together, but they had no child. They prayed and prayed, and finally, they were blessed with a little daughter, who they named Kongjwi. Unfortunately, Kongjwi's mother died when she was still a very young child.

For a time, Kongjwi's father remained a widower and looked after little Kongjwi by himself. But as the little girl grew, the magistrate thought it might be best for her to have a mother teach her what she needed to know, so he began to look for a new wife. Eventually, he married a widow who had a daughter herself, a little girl named Patjwi, who was about the same age as Kongjwi. At first, everything went well, but once Kongjwi's stepmother had established herself as the lady of the house, she began to mistreat Kongjwi. She never did this when Kongjwi's father was home, but only when he had gone out on business or visited friends. Kongjwi bore this all bravely because she knew her father loved her, and she didn't want to upset him with tales about how she was being treated.

Not long after Kongjwi's father remarried, Kongjwi's fortunes truly turned for the worst. Kongjwi's father died, leaving poor Kongjwi with no other family than her cruel stepmother and stepsister. Kongjwi's stepmother turned her stepdaughter into a servant, forcing her to do laundry, tend the garden, clean and cook the rice, and do many other tasks. Patjwi, on the other hand, was treated as though she were a princess. She never had to do any work. She had the finest clothes and ate the finest foods. And she followed her mother's lead in her behavior, also treating poor Kongjwi very badly indeed.

One day, Kongjwi's stepmother handed her a wooden hoe and demanded that she go to the farthest field from the house and dig up all the weeds. Kongjwi dutifully took the hoe and went to the field, but there were so many stones in the soil that she had barely pulled any weeds at all by midday. Kongjwi saw how little she had accomplished after so much work and began to cry.

"I can't go home until the whole field is clear of weeds," she sobbed, "but I don't see how I will ever finish this."

As she was crying, Kongjwi heard the footsteps of a large animal approaching behind her. She turned around and saw a large black cow.

"Don't be afraid, small one," the cow said. "Tell me why you are crying."

"My stepmother wants me to clear this whole field of weeds, but she only gave me a wooden hoe, and the ground is so full of rocks that I can't make any progress. If I go home without finishing the field, I won't be given anything to eat."

"Never fear. I will help you."

The cow then broke up the ground for Kongjwi and pulled all the weeds. Then she dipped her head and lowed, and a basket full of delicious food appeared.

"Oh, thank you!" Kongjwi cried, but before she could say anything else, the cow vanished.

Kongjwi ran home with the basket full of food.

"Look what the black cow gave me!" she said to her stepmother and stepsister. "Come and have some of this delicious food. The cow even weeded the field for me!"

But instead of being grateful, Kongjwi's stepmother was suspicious. "Why are you telling such lies? Where did you steal that food? You no-account girl, I sent you to weed the field, but instead, you went out taking food from other people, and then you make up stories! Go to your room right now, and don't come out until tomorrow morning!"

Kongjwi tearfully obeyed her stepmother and went to her room.

The stepmother, for her part, shared out the food between herself and her daughter. She may have accused Kongjwi of stealing the food, but she had no intention of making an effort to find who it belonged to and instead gobbled down her share.

The next day, there was to be a festival in the village. Patjwi and her mother dressed in their finest clothes and prepared to leave.

Kongjwi said, "Please, stepmother, may I also go to the festival?"

"Certainly," the stepmother replied, "after you have filled this clay water jar and hulled all the rice in those sacks."

Then the stepmother and Patjwi left the house and went to the festival, leaving poor Kongjwi all alone with two impossible tasks that she had no hope of finishing before the festival was well over. Kongjwi decided to try to hull the rice, at least. So she brought it outside and poured it out on the hulling mats, but there was so much rice, and it was taking so long that she was sure she would not finish before her stepmother and stepsister came home. Kongjwi sank to the floor, weeping.

"Oh, dear, oh, dear," she cried. "I will never fill that jar, and I will never hull that rice. What am I to do?"

As Kongjwi sat weeping, a flock of sparrows settled in the tree next to her. Suddenly, the little birds flew down onto the hulling mats and began pecking at the rice. Kongjwi nearly began to shoo them away, but soon she saw that the sparrows were hulling the rice for her. With the industrious little birds' help, Kongjwi soon had all the rice clean and ready to be cooked.

"Thank you for all your help," Kongjwi said to the sparrows. "But I wish you could fix the water jug for me, too, little birds."

Just then, a voice said, "I can help you with the jug."

Kongjwi turned around and around to see who was speaking, but there appeared to be no one there. Then Kongjwi looked down near her feet, and there she saw the owner of the voice. Now, some say that this was a bee, while others say that it was a toad or *tokgabi*, a little imp that sometimes lives in people's houses. But whichever creature it was doesn't matter as much as the fact that it helped to plug the hole in the jug so that when Kongjwi filled it, the water stayed inside, just as it was supposed to do.

Kongjwi went to the festival, where she met her stepmother and stepsister.

"What are you doing here?" the stepmother demanded. "I told you that you couldn't come to the festival until you finished all your work."

"Oh, but it is finished, stepmother," Kongjwi replied. "A flock of sparrows helped me hull the rice, and a little creature helped mend the water jug."

At once, the stepmother began to beat Kongjwi. "You little liar! You tell such tales! Go home right now! I don't want to see your face until morning!"

And so, poor Kongjwi had to leave the festival in shame, and she wept all the way home.

When the stepmother and stepsister arrived home, they saw that the work had indeed been done just as Kongjwi said, but instead of feeling ashamed of themselves and apologizing, they just made themselves a good dinner and then went to bed.

A few weeks later, there was another celebration in the village. Again, Kongjwi asked permission to go, and again, her stepmother gave her an impossible task.

"Yes, you can go," the stepmother said, "as soon as you have woven all that flaxen thread into linen and all that silken thread into silk."

Kongjwi saw the huge piles of thread and despaired. There was no way she would be able to finish all of that in time, but she had no choice but to try.

After her stepmother and stepsister had left the house, Kongjwi picked up a skein of flaxen thread and set up her loom. Soon, she was weaving away, making good cloth quickly, for Kongjwi was a practiced weaver. Once she had finished the first piece of cloth, she looked again at the skeins of thread and began to weep.

"Oh, dear, oh, dear," she cried. "I shall never finish weaving all of that. I shall never go to the celebration, and surely my stepmother will beat me when she returns, no matter how much fine cloth I have woven."

As Kongjwi sat there weeping, she heard a soft, lowing sound coming from outside. She opened the door, and who should be there but her friend, the black cow.

"Tell me what is wrong," the cow said.

"I have to weave all that thread into cloth so that I can go to the celebration, but I will never finish it, and my stepmother will beat me when she comes home," Kongjwi said.

"Never fear. I will help you."

The cow dipped its head and lowed three times, and suddenly in the place of all the skeins of thread were several bolts of the finest linen and silken cloth.

Kongjwi was beside herself with joy.

"Oh, thank you, thank you, honorable cow," she said and bowed low.

"What else do you need, child?"

"I don't want to ask for more when you have already done so much."

"It is of no matter. Please, tell me what other help you need."

"May I have a new suit of clothes to wear to the celebration? Even my best clothes are just rags."

"Certainly."

The cow bowed its head and lowed once more, and Kongjwi found herself clad in a beautiful silk gown with matching silk slippers. Kongjwi bowed to the cow and thanked it again, and then the cow vanished.

Kongjwi began to walk to the celebration in high spirits, but her spirits sank as soon as she caught sight of her stepmother and stepsister. They were staring at Kongjwi with their mouths open, but then the stepmother closed her mouth and set her face into an angry frown. She began striding toward Kongjwi.

When Kongjwi saw this, she knew that she was in for yet another beating, so she turned around and ran away. Not paying much attention to where she was going, she ran right past a young government official, and as Kongjwi passed him, one of her slippers fell off. The official had seen the slipper fall. He asked one of his servants to pick it up so that they might try to find its owner. They went into the village and presented the slipper to everyone, but no one seemed to know who it belonged to.

Finally, the official approached Patjwi and her mother.

"Is this your slipper?" the official asked.

Patjwi saw how handsome the young official was and thought that if she could convince him that it was her slipper, he might look favorably on her.

"It's mine," she said. "It's the one I lost a little while ago."

The official was skeptical, for this young woman didn't look at all like the one he had seen drop the shoe.

But then again, he thought, *I might be mistaken, and it would be wrong not to give the slipper back.*

Then he said to Patjwi, "If the slipper is truly yours, it should fit you. Please try it on."

Patjwi attempted to put on the slipper, but try as she might, she could not make it fit. Patjwi's lie made the magistrate very angry, and he ordered that Patjwi be punished. Then he asked whether the slipper belonged to anyone else.

The stepmother said, "I think it is mine."

So, the official had her try on the slipper herself, but again it did not fit, and the official had the stepmother punished as well.

The official then told his servants to go throughout the district to find the slipper's true owner. They went from house to house until the sun had nearly gone down, and still, they had not found the owner.

Finally, they went to Kongjwi's house. They knocked on the door and presented the slipper. Kongjwi, who had changed back into her rags, answered the door and asked what the men wanted.

"Is this your slipper?" they asked as they showed her the slipper.

"Yes, it is mine," Kongjwi replied. "It fell off when I was running today."

"Will you try it on, please? We need to be sure it is yours."

Kongjwi tried on the slipper, and it fit perfectly. The servants were very happy, not least because they were very tired and wanted to go home.

"Come and speak to our employer," they said. "He was the one who sent us to find you."

Kongjwi went with the men to meet the official.

The men said, "Here is the young woman who lost the slipper."

The official was smitten by Kongjwi's beauty, but he was confused by her coarse and well-patched gown.

"Are you sure?" the official asked the servants. "The woman I saw was richly dressed, but this one is in rags."

Kongjwi bowed to the official. "Honorable sir, truly it is I. I had to hide my good clothes from my stepmother and stepsister because they are cruel and likely would have torn them to shreds. But it was I you saw running past you. I was running away from my stepmother and was so frightened I didn't notice I had lost my slipper until I got home."

"Very well," the official said. "Please try on the slipper. I need to know for sure that you are the rightful owner."

Kongjwi tried on the slipper, and again, it fitted perfectly.

"If your honor pleases," she said, "I can go home and change into my good clothes, and then you will know for sure that it was I you saw earlier today."

The official agreed, so he and his servants accompanied Kongjwi to her home. The official waited outside while Kongjwi went in to change. The stepmother and stepsister were still recovering from the punishment they had received, so they remained hidden in their rooms when they heard the official arrive.

Soon, Kongjwi came out of the house dressed in the finery that the cow had given her.

"Yes, it truly was you I saw," the official said, "and I must confess, I fell in love with you at that moment. Will you consent to be my wife?"

"Oh, yes!" Kongjwi replied, for she had fallen in love with the handsome official.

And so it was that Kongjwi married very well, and she lived happily with her husband until the end of her days. And the stepmother and stepsister? Well, Kongjwi saw to it that they were well provided for because she had a good heart and couldn't bear to see anyone suffering.

The Faithful Daughter

The story of Sim Chung and her father, Sim Hyun, contains three important elements of Korean culture and folklore: the dutiful child who makes sacrifices to help an aging parent, helpful Buddhist monks, and water dragons. Sim Chung's sacrifice is an example of filial piety, a concept and practice central to many Asian cultures. Filial piety has long been an important part of Korean culture and systems of morality. It also has many roots in the teachings of Confucius, the Chinese scholar and sage who lived between 551 and 479 BCE.

Once there was an old man named Sim Hyun, who had a lovely daughter named Sim Chung. Sim Hyun and Sim Chung lived together in a little cottage, which was sparsely furnished because they were very poor. Sim Hyun could no longer work because he was blind, and Chung's mother had died not long after Chung was born. For a time, Chung's father had provided for his little family by selling the many precious things he owned, but one day he realized he had sold everything and had no other prospects. Sim Hyun, therefore, became a beggar, and every day Chung would go out with him to guide him.

But all of this changed when Chung reached the age of womanhood, for respectable women never went about in public but rather stayed at home. Since the only way that Sim Hyun knew to provide for his family was to beg, he continued going out every day to seek alms, a task made even more difficult by the absence of his dear daughter.

One day, Sim Hyun went out to beg as usual, but as he was walking home, he lost his way and fell into a deep ditch. Sim Hyun had nearly despaired of ever getting out of the ditch when he felt strong hands grasping his arms and pulling him back onto the road.

"Thank you, thank you!" Sim Hyun said. "Who is it that I have to thank for this rescue?"

"I am a priest at the Buddhist temple," the man replied. "I also have a message for you: If you bring three hundred bags of rice to the temple, your sight will be restored to you."

The priest then went on his way, and Sim Hyun resumed his walk home. At first, he was elated to think that he might see again, but then he began to think of the task he had to complete, and he despaired.

I am so poor, he thought. *How will I ever get three hundred bags of rice? I think that priest was mocking me, despite him pulling me out of that ditch.*

Sim Hyun got home safely. He told Chung about his misadventure in the ditch and the Buddhist monk who had rescued him.

"But I have no idea how to get that much rice," Sim Hyun wailed. "I want to repay the monk for his kindness and get my sight back, but how can I buy so much rice on the alms I manage to beg?"

"Don't worry, Father," Sim Chung said. "I'm sure I'll think of something. We'll get the rice, and you'll get your sight back. All that's needed is patience and a bit of cleverness."

That night, Chung had a dream. Chung's mother appeared and told the young woman what she needed to do to get the rice.

In the morning, Chung said to her father, "I think I know how to get the rice, but I will have to be gone for some time. Can you manage without me until I come back?"

"I think so," Sim Hyun replied. "I know that you are both strong and clever, and I trust you to do the right thing."

Chung then cooked a lot of food for her father to eat while she was gone. Next, she put on a gray robe, a big hat, and a white veil across her face so that people would think she was in mourning. After bowing at her mother's grave in thanks for the dream, Chung set out to carry out her plan.

As she had been directed by her dream, Chung walked to the home of a rich merchant. This merchant dealt in rice and was famous for the trading he did in China. But recently, his fortunes had turned because the River Dragon barred the way, preventing the ships from sailing, and the only thing the Dragon would accept in payment to open the waters again was the sacrifice of a beautiful young woman. So desperate was the merchant that he had made it known that he would pay three hundred bags of rice to anyone who could get the Dragon to leave him alone.

When Sim Chung arrived at the house of the merchant, she told him her whole story.

"I do not want you to die," the merchant said. "You are such a dutiful daughter. You should go back home."

"I can't go back home without the rice," Chung said, "and this is the only way I can get it. Let me sacrifice myself so that my father can get his sight back."

The merchant loaded one hundred and fifty horses with the three hundred sacks of rice and sent them to the temple. When Chung presented the rice to the priest who had helped her father, he thanked her very kindly.

The priest then said, "You need to know that your father's sight might not come back right away. It might take some time, even several years. But it will come back, never fear."

Chung went back home to tell her father that the rice had been delivered. Then she made arrangements for some kindly neighbors to look after the old man. That done, Chung dressed in the lovely bridal garments the merchant had given her, and then she went down to the harbor to take the ship to her doom. The ship set sail and no sooner had the sight of land disappeared behind them than the waters began to roil and churn.

"This is the place where the River Dragon lives," the merchant said. "If you're determined to go through with this, you must jump into the water here."

Sim Chung gathered all her courage and jumped into the swirling water. Immediately the waters calmed, and the ships could continue their journey as though nothing at all had happened. Meanwhile, under the water, Sim Chung found herself sinking lower and lower. She soon lost consciousness, thinking that she would never see the light of day again, but eventually, she awoke and found herself in a beautiful underwater palace. Servants came to bid her welcome and then conducted her to meet the River Dragon himself. When Chung came into the Dragon's presence, she bowed very low.

"I am not worthy of being here in your palace," Chung said. "Do with me as you wish."

"You are most worthy," the Dragon said, "for you were willing to give your life so that your father might have his sight back. I wish you to be my guest for a time. Have no fear. All your needs will be met."

The River Dragon was true to his word. Servants prepared delicious meals for Chung and gave her the most beautiful clothes to wear.

Several days passed, and then the River Dragon said, "It is time for you to go back to your own world."

The Dragon placed Chung inside a lotus, which rose up, up, up from the bottom of the sea to float on the gently rocking waves at the surface. Not long afterward, who should sail by but the merchant who had given Chung the rice. He saw the lotus and bade his sailors to bring his ship close to the beautiful flower.

"This is the most beautiful lotus I have ever seen," the merchant said. "We should take it to the king."

The sailors duly brought the flower on board and took it directly to the palace. The king was enchanted by the lovely blossom and rewarded the merchant and his crew very well. Then the king put the lotus in a pond in his own garden, thinking himself the most fortunate king of all to have such a flower in his palace.

Now, Chung did not spend all her time inside the flower. At night, she would come out and wander about the king's gardens. She managed to do this entirely unseen by anyone in the palace until one night, the king found himself restless and went for a walk in the garden. There he saw the most beautiful maiden he had ever seen, and he instantly fell in love with her.

When Chung realized she had been spotted, she tried to go back into the lotus but found that it had sunk back down under the water.

"Don't be afraid," the king said to Chung. "I won't hurt you. I have never seen a maiden as lovely as you, and I would like you to be my wife."

Chung assented and the king conducted her to his royal apartments where she was given a fine meal and many beautiful robes to wear. The king, for his part, went to visit his wise men to ask whether the marriage would be a fortunate one.

"Oh, yes, indeed, this is a most auspicious match," the wise men said. "You see, when the merchant brought you the lotus for your garden, a new star appeared in the sky. Heaven itself approves of this match, so you must marry the girl as soon as you are able."

The king, therefore, commanded that preparations for the wedding be made, and on the appointed day, he and Chung were married with much pomp and rejoicing. The young couple was very happy together, but sometimes, Chung felt sad because she missed her father.

One day, the king noticed that Chung was not her usual cheerful self. "What is wrong, my wife? What can I do to make you happy again? It hurts my heart to see you in sorrow this way."

"It is nothing," Chung replied. "I just miss my father. That is all."

"Well, then we must bring him here. Tell me where I may find him."

"I don't know how to get there from here. And my father is blind. I don't know how he would get here by himself."

"I know what we'll do. I'll send out my servants to round up all the blind people in the kingdom. We'll give them a wonderful feast, and you can show me which man your father is. And if he consents, he can live here in the palace with us."

Chung agreed that this was a good plan and thanked her husband most gratefully.

On the day of the feast, Chung looked at each blind person who came to the palace, but none of them was her father. She began to wonder whether he had passed away when a last, straggling latecomer appeared. Chung's heart leaped, for who should this be than her own beloved father!

Chung ran to embrace him, but Sim Hyun pulled away.

"Who is this that is embracing me?" he asked.

"It is I, Sim Chung," Chung replied. "It is your own dear daughter. I live here in the palace now. The king is my husband."

"I don't believe it. I think someone is playing a trick on me. My daughter sacrificed herself to the River Dragon a long time ago. I won't believe that you're really her unless I see your face."

Just then, Sim Hyun's sight returned, and when he beheld his beautiful daughter dressed in the robes of a queen, his legs gave way beneath him. Chung and the king helped the old man up, and the king ordered his servants to prepare quarters for him and give him fresh clothing. Sim Hyun lived happily in a house next to the palace. The king made him a trusted official and married him to a good woman who looked after him very well until the end of his days.

Hungbu and Nolbu

The tale of the brothers Hungbu and Nolbu draws on the common trope of the good brother and the bad brother. As with other tales that rely on this trope, the good brother is rewarded by magical beings for his kindness and generosity, while the bad brother attempts to gain the reward by cheating, leading to his downfall. Unlike many Western iterations of this trope, the Korean tale of Hungbu and Nolbu ends with Nolbu, the bad brother, admitting to his wrong behavior and turning his life around. The story thus ends with a balanced relationship between the brothers, who then also share a balanced social and economic status, unlike in similar Western stories where the fortunate, good sibling might reward their conniving, abusive brother or sister but without the bad sibling repenting of their behavior, or where the bad sibling simply disappears from the story altogether in a haze of shame and misfortune.

A long time ago, there were two brothers named Hungbu and Nolbu. Nolbu was the elder, and he was very rich. He lived in a fine house and wore fine clothes. His wife and children lacked for nothing. But despite having so much, Nolbu was a greedy man who always wanted more.

Hungbu was completely unlike his brother. Where Nolbu was rich, Hungbu was poor. Where Nolbu lived in a fine house with a tiled roof, Hungbu lived in a hut with a thatched roof that was always leaking in one spot or another. And where Nolbu's wife and children wanted for nothing, Hungbu's wife and children were clad in rags and rarely had enough to eat.

Now, one would think that Nolbu would have shared his good fortune with his brother, at least, but he refused.

"My fortune is mine," he said. "Let others look after their own."

This was another way that Nolbu was different from his brother, for Hungbu was always happy to help others whenever he could. No kindness was too small for Hungbu to perform.

One of the things that gave Hungbu's miserable life a bit of joy was the swallows' annual flight. Hungbu loved watching the birds as they swooped through the sky. He built a nesting box in the little tree next to his house and was very pleased indeed on the day when he found that a swallow had built a nest and laid her eggs there. When the eggs finally hatched, Hungbu would watch the swallow parents bringing food to their gangly chicks. It was very pleasant to watch the little bird family grow.

Finally, the swallow chicks were fledged and nearly ready to leave the nest, but before they could go out into the world, a serpent climbed the tree and swallowed them, one by one, and there was nothing the chicks' frantic parents could do about it. Hungbu arrived just in time to see one of the chicks fall out of the nest just before the serpent got to it. Hungbu ran to save the chick, which had injured its leg in the fall. He took the chick into the house and showed it to his wife.

"Oh, the poor thing," Hungbu's wife said. "Whatever happened?"

"A serpent got into the tree," Hungbu replied. "It ate up all this little fellow's brothers and sisters, and he fell out of the nest. The fall saved his life, but he's hurt and needs help."

Hungbu and his wife found some medicine to put on the little bird's leg, and they gently splinted it with a bit of twig and some thread. The children took it in turns to feed the chick and see that he was warm and comfortable. The chick grew and learned to fly, and when autumn came, the chick joined his flock and flew away with them. Hungbu and his family were sad to see their little friend go, but they were happy that he was now free.

Winter came and went, and when spring returned, so did the swallows. The chick that Hungbu had helped was now a full-grown bird, and he remembered Hungbu's kindness. He flew into the tree next to Hungbu's house and began to chirp and sing. Hungbu looked outside and saw his little friend sitting in the tree.

He ran outside and said, "Greetings, little one. It is good to see you again. I hope you had a fine winter."

In answer, the swallow dropped a gourd seed at Hungbu's feet and then flew away.

That's very odd, Hungbu thought, *but one ought not to spurn a gift from a friend, however small.*

Hungbu showed the seed to his wife. She agreed that it was strange and also that they should treat the gift respectfully.

"Why don't you plant it in the garden?" she said. "I think that would be the best thanks you could give."

Hungbu agreed and planted the seed among the other vegetables growing in his garden. He tended the seed with care, and soon it began to sprout. It soon became apparent that this was no ordinary gourd plant. It grew at ten times the rate of any other plant in the garden. It grew so quickly that it was only a matter of days before it blossomed, and then only a few more days passed before it bore five large gourds.

Hungbu and his wife stood in the garden, staring at the gourds.

"Our little friend gave us a gift indeed," Hungbu said, "but I wonder what we should do with these gourds."

"Let's pick one and cut it open," Hungbu's wife replied. "Maybe that will tell us what we should do next."

This seemed to be the best plan, so Hungbu picked one of the gourds and began to cut it in half. But no sooner had the knife pierced the skin of the gourd than the rice began streaming out.

"Quick! Get something to catch the rice," Hungbu shouted.

Hungbu's wife and children brought vessel after vessel out of the house. They soon had collected enough rice to fill ten large sacks, but even then, there was more rice left over.

"Well, you were right about this being a good gift," Hungbu's wife said. "Let's see what comes out of the next one."

Hungbu picked another gourd and thrust his knife into it. This time a shower of gold coins came out of the gourd. Hungbu and his family collected up all the gold, laughing and shouting with joy.

"We're rich now, Papa!" the children said, to whom Hungbu had told the story of the swallow bringing him the seed. "Your swallow friend is a good friend."

"Yes, he is a good friend, and that's because I was kind to him," Hungbu said. "We need to remember to be kind to everyone, even little birds. Now, shall we open another gourd?"

Everyone cheered at this, and so Hungbu picked another gourd and started to slice it. This time a beautiful fairy came out of the gourd.

She turned to the two gourds that were still on the vine and sang, "Come out! Come out!"

One of the gourds fell off the vine and split in two when it hit the ground. Inside was a blue bottle. Then the other gourd fell and split, and inside that one was a red bottle.

Both of the bottles said, "Here I am!"

The fairy said to the bottles, "You have a job to do. Build a beautiful mansion for this family."

The blue bottle quivered, and then carpenters began streaming out of it. The red bottle quivered, and then timber and bricks and tiles began pouring out of it. The carpenters took the building materials, and in no time, they had constructed a lovely house for Hungbu and his family. When the work was done, the carpenters went back into their bottle, and the fairy disappeared.

Hungbu and his family were overjoyed. They now had a fine house that was warm and had a roof that didn't leak. They wore fine clothes and never went hungry.

It didn't take long for Nolbu to notice the reversal of his brother's fortunes. But instead of rejoicing that his brother was doing well, Nolbu was jealous.

How dare he get rich right under my nose! Nolbu thought. *I'm going to ask him how he managed it.*

Nolbu went to Hungbu's house and was welcomed as a guest should be.

Once greetings had been exchanged, Nolbu said, "This is a very fine house, and you seem to be doing very well. It's also rather sudden. How did you do it?"

Hungbu then told Nolbu how he had saved the injured chick and how the chick had returned the following spring with the gift of the gourd seed.

Ha! Nolbu thought. *Anybody can patch up a hurt bird. I'm going to do the same thing. Easy money. Then I'll be the rich one again!*

Nolbu built a nest box in the tree outside his house. He waited until a swallow made a nest, laid her eggs, and watched for the day when the chicks were fledged. When the day came, Nolbu snatched one unlucky chick from the nest and dashed it to the ground. He bound up the chick's injured leg and replaced it in the nest. Autumn came, and the chick flew south with the rest of his flock. Spring came, and the chick returned, perching itself on the tree where Nolbu had built the nest.

Nolbu saw that the chick had returned.

He rubbed his hands together and said, "Aha! It worked. Time to get more gold!"

He went outside. The swallow saw him, dropped a seed at his feet, and flew away. Nolbu planted the seed and tended it. The gourd plant grew just as quickly as Hungbu's had done, and when the gourds were finally ripe, Nolbu went out with a sharp knife, grinning with glee over what a large fortune he was about to have. He picked a gourd and plunged the knife into it, but instead of gold, a stream of little imps came out. Each imp had a stick in its hand.

The leader of the imps said, "We are here to punish you for your greed."

Then the imps set upon Nolbu and beat him black and blue. After their work was done, the imps disappeared.

"Well, that was most unfortunate," Nolbu said when he had his breath back. "Maybe the next gourd has some gold in it."

Nolbu cut into another gourd, but this one was full of debt collectors.

"You must hand over everything you have," the debt collectors said.

They did not leave until Nolbu had not one small coin to his name, and he and his family had been thrown out of their house with just the clothes on their backs.

"Whatever happened to our house and our money and our belongings?" Nolbu's wife cried. "What have you done?"

"Well, I saw how Hungbu got rich so quickly," Nolbu replied, "so I'm trying the same thing he did, but it hasn't been working right. I'll try one more gourd. There has to be gold in that one!"

Nolbu picked another gourd and cut it open. Out of this gourd streamed the filthiest, most brackish water anyone has ever seen. Nolbu threw the gourd to the ground and ran to Hungbu's house, his clothing covered in filth and his body covered in bruises from the beating the imps had given him.

"Help me! Help me!" Nolbu cried. "I've lost everything! My family has no home! Help me!"

Hungbu came running out of the house when he heard Nolbu's cries.

"Whatever is the matter, brother?" Hungbu asked. "How can I help you?"

Nolbu told Hungbu the story of the swallow and the gourd.

"I understand now what I did wrong," Nolbu said. "I have lived a bad life. I was never kind or generous. I should have helped you when you were poor, but I didn't. I beg your forgiveness and ask you to help me and my family, even though I don't deserve your kindness."

"Never fear, brother," Hungbu said. "I'll make sure everything is set right."

Hungbu shared all his wealth with his brother and built a new home for Nolbu and his family. Nolbu became kind and generous to everyone he met, and he and his brother lived happily for the end of their days.

Part IV: Dragons, Spirits, and Heavenly Beings

The Heavenly Lovers

In her rendering of this old Korean folktale, author Janie Jaehyun Park notes that the two main characters, the farmer Kyonu and the weaver Jingnyo, represent the stars Altair and Vega. These two stars are in the constellations of Aquila and Lyra, respectively, and on summer nights, they each shine brightly on opposite sides of the Milky Way. This tale is a just-so story about the these two stars' positions, the plumage of magpies, and the origins of summer rain and summer drought.

The Kingdom of Heaven was a very fine place. Everyone was happy, and everyone did their duties. There was plenty to eat and many fine clothes to wear. Food was plentiful because Kyonu, the plowman, was so good at farming and taking care of his oxen. Clothing was beautiful because Jingnyo, the weaver, was so good at weaving silk into beautiful cloth. Everyone praised Kyonu and Jingnyo for their hard work and the good food and beautiful cloth they provided.

One day, as Kyonu was driving his oxen to the field, he passed by Jingnyo's house. Kyonu happened to look through the window and see Jingnyo at her loom. Jingnyo happened to look out the window just as Kyonu paused to watch her at her work. The two young people gazed upon one another, and instantly they fell deeply in love. They asked the King of Heaven for his permission to marry. The king gave them his blessing, and soon they were wed.

Kyonu and Jingnyo were very happy together. In fact, they were so happy that they spent all their time together. Instead of plowing the fields and farming, Kyonu went for walks in the park with Jingnyo. Instead of weaving beautiful cloth, Jingnyo prepared picnics and went out into the countryside to spend the day with Kyonu. They took walks and had picnics, and on rainy days they spent their time together inside the house. Soon the Kingdom of Heaven began to run out of food and good clothes because Kyonu was not farming and Jingnyo was not weaving.

The people of the kingdom went to the King of Heaven and said, "O noble King of Heaven, we are starving and freezing because Kyonu will not plow and Jingnyo will not weave. Please do something to get them to go back to their duties, or we will all surely die."

The King of Heaven went to Kyonu and commanded him to take his oxen and go plow the fields. Then he went to Jingnyo and commanded her to take up her shuttle and begin weaving. Kyonu and Jingnyo both went back to their work, but they didn't do it very well; they both spent most of their time thinking about the other and wishing they could be together.

The King of Heaven saw that he was not being obeyed and became very angry. He sent Kyonu to the farthest east and Jingnyo to the farthest west.

"If you cannot do your duties when you are together, then you must live separately," the King of Heaven said.

Kyonu and Jingnyo cried and pleaded with the king to let them stay together, but the king refused.

"I will grant you one respite," he said. "Every year, on the seventh day of the seventh month, you may see each other, but you must each stay on your own side of the Great River of Heaven, which some call the Milky Way."

Kyonu and Jingnyo bade one another a tearful farewell. Kyonu went to the east with his oxen, where he plowed as he used to do, and Jingnyo went to the west with her loom and thread, where she wove as she used to do. Soon the Kingdom of Heaven had enough food and enough clothes, but Kyonu and Jingnyo were sad and missed one other terribly. They performed their duties, but all they could think of was how good it would be to see one another again.

Finally, the seventh day of the seventh month arrived. Kyonu and Jingnyo were each on their own side of the Great River of Heaven.

"Come over to my side," Kyonu cried.

"I can't. The river is too wide," Jingnyo said. "You need to come over to my side."

But Kyonu couldn't cross the river either. The two lovers were so saddened by this that they began to shed bitter tears, which fell to the earth as rain. Kyonu and Jingnyo cried so much and for so long that the earth began to flood. Houses and trees were being washed away, and people and animals were drowning in the swirling, deepening waters.

The animals and birds held a council to see what might be done.

They discussed many different plans, but none of them seemed likely to work until the magpies said, "Leave it to us."

The magpies flew up to heaven in a flurry of black feathers. They arranged themselves wing to wing and head to tail until they had made a living bridge that spanned the Great River. Kyonu and Jingnyo raced to the middle of the bridge, where they embraced one another with much joy. The two lovers wept as they embraced, but this time, their tears fell as good, gentle rain, the kind that makes the crops grow and refreshes the earth. Kyonu and Jingnyo stayed together as long as possible, but soon the time came for them to part.

And so, every year, on the seventh day of the seventh month, the two lovers come to the same places on the Great River of Heaven, and the magpies make a bridge for them so that they can meet. On the earth below, it rains whenever Kyonu and Jingnyo have met and are weeping lovers' tears, and there is a drought when they meet and do not weep. The heads of magpies are also bald because Kyonu and Jingnyo step on them as they mount the bridge.

The Woodcutter and the Heavenly Maiden

This story draws on two common tropes: rewards for kindness to a being in distress and the consequences of breaking a taboo. Here, the woodcutter is rewarded for helping a mountain god in the form of a deer elude a hunter. The deer helps the woodcutter get a heavenly maiden for his bride, but then the woodcutter loses his wife when he forgets to follow the rules the deer gave him at the outset. In this particular iteration of these tropes, the woodcutter breaks the taboo not through hubris but rather through compassion for his wife's sadness. A second taboo later in the story is broken by sheer accident, leading to the woodcutter being permanently separated from his family.

Translator James H. Grayson notes in comments on his version of the tale that it is one of the most common stories told throughout Korea and first written down in the early twentieth century—although it is much older. There are multiple variants of the story; the one that Grayson presents ends happily, with the woodcutter living in heaven with his wife and children, but other versions, including the one presented below, end in misfortune and sorrow.

There was once a woodcutter who went up the mountainside every day to cut a load of wood. He would tie the wood into bundles and then bring it down into the village to sell. One day, as the woodcutter went about his work, he heard the sound of delicate hoofbeats and panting breath. The woodcutter turned, and there he saw a deer running in his direction.

"Quick! Hide me!" the deer said. "A hunter is after me, and he will surely kill me if he catches me!"

The woodcutter quickly helped the deer conceal itself in some nearby bushes. Not long afterward, the hunter came running up.

"Have you seen a deer run by here?" the hunter asked.

"Yes," the woodcutter replied. "It bounded off that way."

The hunter gave the woodcutter his thanks and then ran off in the direction the woodcutter had indicated.

When the hunter was gone, the deer came out of the bushes.

"Thank you for saving my life," it said. "I am the god of this mountain, and I wish to repay your kindness. Ask me anything, and it shall be yours."

Now, for some time, the woodcutter had been feeling lonely and wished he had a wife, so he said, "I would like a lovely wife, please, honorable one."

"It shall be as you ask, if you follow my instructions," the deer said. "Go to the pond that is in the pass just above us. That is where the heavenly maidens come to bathe every morning. Their dresses hold the wings they use to fly between heaven and earth. Steal the dress of one of the maidens. When she asks for it back, tell her that you will give it back if she consents to be your wife. But under no circumstances must you let her see the dress until after you have had four children together."

In the morning, the woodcutter went to the pond the deer had told him about. He concealed himself in some bushes near the pond and waited. Soon he heard the sound of women's voices and laughter. Several heavenly maidens came flying down and landed on the soft grass near the pond. They took off their winged dresses and went into the cool water to bathe. The woodcutter took hold of the nearest dress and stealthily pulled it into the bushes.

When the maidens were done bathing, they put on their dresses and flew back up into heaven, all but one of them, who looked frantically around the edges of the pond for her dress. It was nowhere to be seen, and she began to cry.

That was when the woodcutter came out of the bushes and said, "Don't be sad, lovely maiden. I know where your dress is. I'll give it back if you consent to be my wife."

The heavenly maiden liked the look of the woodcutter, who was strong and tall and seemed kind.

"Yes, I will marry you," she said.

The woodcutter then gave the maiden a different dress that he had brought for her to wear and left the heavenly dress where he had hidden it. He brought the maiden home to meet his mother, and soon the two women were chatting like old friends. In the morning, the woodcutter went to retrieve the dress, which he placed in an old chest in his mother's house. The maiden and the woodcutter were soon married in a joyful ceremony, and they lived together quite happily.

After several years, the woodcutter and his wife were the proud parents of three beautiful children. One day, the woodcutter came home from his work and found his wife sitting by the hearth, staring sadly into the flames.

"What is wrong, my wife?" he asked. "You seem sad."

"I am sad," she replied. "I haven't seen my sisters or the rest of my family for a long time, and I miss them. Also, I miss my heavenly, winged dress. It was so beautiful, and I loved wearing it so much. I wish I could see it again, just once."

The woodcutter felt sorry for his wife, so he brought out the dress and gave it to her, forgetting that the deer had told him to wait until they had had four children together. No sooner had the woodcutter's wife put on the dress than she picked up her three children and flew away into heaven.

"Come back," the woodcutter shouted. "Please don't leave me! Please don't take away my children!"

But his wife was already too far away to hear his cries.

The next day, the grieving woodcutter went to work as usual because he didn't know what else to do. As he was cutting up a tree he had just felled, he heard soft hoofbeats behind him. He turned and saw the deer he had helped years earlier.

"You gave her the dress, didn't you?" the deer asked.

"Yes, I did," the woodcutter replied. "She seemed so sad, and I just wanted to make her happy again. I didn't know that she'd fly away and take our children with her. I wish I could go up to heaven to see her again."

"If you go to the pond where you first found her, you can go up to heaven. The heavenly maidens don't come down to bathe anymore, not since you stole the dress. Instead, they lower a bucket down and draw the water up to heaven so that they can bathe there. Go back to the pond, and when the bucket comes down, get into it. They will pull you up into heaven, and you can see your wife and children again."

The woodcutter did as the deer instructed him, and when the bucket came down to scoop up the water, the woodcutter jumped inside. It was a very long ride up to heaven. The woodcutter was terrified the entire way that he would fall out of the bucket and be killed, but he arrived in heaven without mishap and immediately began calling for his wife.

Hearing her husband's voice, the woodcutter's wife came running over to where he was standing, followed by their three children. It was a joyous reunion, for the wife and the children had also missed the woodcutter. The woodcutter's wife introduced her husband to her family, and they all approved of him and welcomed him.

The woodcutter lived happily in heaven with his wife and children for a time, but soon, he began to miss his mother. When his wife asked why he seemed so glum, the woodcutter explained that he wanted to visit his mother. The woodcutter's wife asked her father to lend the woodcutter a dragon horse so that he could make a visit to earth.

"Certainly," the wife's father said, "but you must not dismount, or else the dragon horse will come straight back here, and you will never be allowed to visit heaven ever again."

The woodcutter said goodbye to his wife and children, promising to come back soon. He mounted the dragon horse, which flew swiftly down to the woodcutter's mother's house. The mother was overjoyed to see her son, whom she had thought dead.

"I've made some squash soup," she said, "just the way you like it. Let me get you a bowl."

The old woman went into the house, and soon, she came back out with a bowl full of steaming, fragrant soup. She handed the bowl to her son, but when he took it, some of the hot soup splashed on his hand, making him drop the bowl. As the bowl fell, some of the hot soup splashed onto the back of the dragon horse. The dragon horse reared and bucked, throwing the woodcutter off its back. Then the dragon horse flew away into heaven.

The woodcutter lived the rest of his life with his mother, and when he died, his spirit turned into a rooster. And when the rooster lifts its beak to the sky and crows, it is the spirit of the woodcutter calling to his wife and children, who he still misses to this very day.

Lady Suro and the Sea Dragon

As with other dragons in this volume, the one that kidnaps Lady Suro is a creature of the waters. Author Kichung Kim suggests that Lord Sunjong and his wife begin their journey in the city of Kyongju, the capital of the kingdom of Silla on the southwestern coast of the Korean Peninsula. Kangnung likewise is on the coast, so their entire journey would have been made along the seashore.

This legend is set during the reign of King Songdok (702-737 CE) and commemorated by a statue in the modern city of Samcheok, which lies on the coast about two-thirds of the way between Kyongju and Kangnung. The statue is located in a park on the headland. It sits atop a cliff overlooking the sea and represents a richly dressed Lady Suro sitting on the back of the sea dragon, both of them looking out to sea.

When Songdok reigned as king in Korea, Lord Sunjong went on a journey to Kangnung. Sunjong had just been promoted to the office of magistrate, and he was going to Kangnung to perform his duties. As is proper for any nobleman, Sunjong traveled with an entourage of servants. His lovely wife, Suro, also accompanied him.

The journey to Kangnung was a long one, so at noon, the party stopped on a beach to eat the midday meal. Lady Suro got out of her carriage and walked along the beach, smelling the fresh sea air and admiring the cliffs that towered over the beach. Suddenly, she saw something that took her breath away: a bright red flower growing out of a cleft in the cliff face. Suro had never seen anything so lovely.

She went to the servants and said, "Do you see that flower up there? I simply must have it! Which of you will climb up and get it for me?"

The servants looked at the cliff face. They walked back and forth along it, trying to find a way to climb up.

After some minutes, they went back to Lady Suro and said, "Apologies, honorable one, but we cannot climb that cliff face. No one has the skill for that."

Just then, an old man happened by, driving some cattle along the beach. The old man had heard what the servants said and scoffed, thinking them cowardly. The old man went over to the Lady Suro and bowed low. Then he sang this song:

Beautiful lady,
I am here to serve you.
Allow me to leave my cattle here.
I will climb up that cliff
And pluck the flower for you,
If you will accept my service.

Lady Suro gladly agreed, so the man climbed up the cliff face, plucked the flower, and gave it to the lady with another bow. Lady Suro thanked the man, who gathered up his cattle and went on his way. Lord Sunjong was pleased to see his wife so happy, but he knew that they needed to travel onwards if they were going to arrive in Kangnung in a timely way. He commanded the servants to pack up the lunch things, and when everyone had mounted their horses or gotten back into their carriages, the party continued on.

When they reached Imhae Pavilion, which also stood on the seashore, they stopped for another meal. Lady Suro got out of the carriage and wandered a little way down the beach, holding her flower and smelling its fragrance. She hadn't gone far when suddenly the sea began to roil and swirl. A great column of water shot up into the air, and out of it appeared a great sea dragon. The dragon snatched up Lady Suro and then disappeared beneath the waves.

Lord Sunjong cried out in anger and fear. He ran toward the surf but soon realized that there was no way for him to get to his wife.

"Oh, no, oh, no," Sunjong cried. "How am I to get my wife back? How will I ever make the dragon give her back?"

An old man happened to be on the beach at the same time as Lord Sunjong and his party. The old man saw what had happened to Suro and how distraught Sunjong was. The old man went to Sunjong and bowed.

"Honorable sir," the old man said, "is it not true that if many voices sing together, nothing can withstand them? If we sing a song and beat the ground with staves, surely the dragon will be convinced to bring back your lovely wife. Gather up all the people from this district. Give them staves to beat the ground. Have them sing. Then the dragon will be afraid."

Lord Sunjong agreed that this was the best course. Soon all the people from the district were lined up on the beach, and each one had a stout staff made of bamboo in their hands. At the old man's direction, the people began to strike the sand with their staffs, and they sang this song:

Turtle! Turtle! Send back Lady Suro!
She does not belong to you!
Her husband wants her back!
Send back Lady Suro at once,
Or we will come with our fishing nets and catch you,
And then we will slice you up and eat you for supper!

The sound of the singing and the thudding of the staves on the beach reached down, down, down to the bottom of the sea, where the dragon had his palace. The dragon heard the people threatening to eat him, and he was very afraid. He took the Lady Suro and went back to the beach, where he deposited her gently on the sand in front of her husband. Then the dragon went back down to his palace and was never seen again.

"Oh, my dearest wife," Sunjong said. "I am so happy that the dragon brought you back unharmed. Tell us, what was it like under the ocean?"

"It was the most beautiful place I have ever been," Suro replied. "Everything was carved out of precious stones. The food and drink were tastier than the most delicious thing you have ever eaten, and it was unlike any other kind of food I've ever seen."

Everyone listened with rapt attention to Suro's tale. They also noticed a delicate, haunting perfume on her clothing, a scent unlike any other, richer and sweeter than the rarest perfumes on earth.

Now, one might think that such an encounter would be so rare as to not be repeated, but Lady Suro was so beautiful that any time she traveled past a body of water, the resident spirits would snatch her and take her down to their palaces. Each time this happened, Lord Sunjong knew what to do: he assembled all the people of the district and gave them stout bamboo staves and had them sing the song that brought Lady Suro back from the palace of the sea dragon.

Wongwang the Monk

Korean monarchs and military leaders were not the only historical figures to become characters in myths and legends: Buddhist monks also received this honor. One such monk was a man named Wongwang, who lived in the sixth and seventh centuries. Wongwang is credited with having made important religious reforms in the kingdom of Silla, especially with the creation of the Hwarang Troop, an elite military brigade that combined martial training with education in Buddhist philosophy and Confucian precepts. The tale retold below explains how Wongwang came about his knowledge and used it for the greater good.

Once there was a monk named Wongwang. He entered the monastery when he was but a boy, and he was very learned and holy. He liked nothing better than to read Buddhist holy books and works of Confucianism. When he was thirty years old, he decided he'd had enough of living among other human beings. What he wanted was a quiet place all to himself, where he could read and pray and think in peace and solitude. Accordingly, Wongwang made his way up Samgi Mountain, where he found a small cave that was dry and cozy.

"Ah!" Wongwang said. "This is the best place for a hermitage. I shall be very happy here."

Wongwang hadn't lived very long in his hermitage when another monk built himself a small dwelling not far away. Since the other monk kept to himself, Wongwang didn't think much about him. This all changed one night when Wongwang was sitting in his cave reciting scriptures. As he was chanting out the holy words, Wongwang suddenly heard a voice.

"Oh, excellent! You are a very learned and holy monk, just the person I have been looking for!"

Wongwang stopped his chant and looked up. There in his cave stood a spirit.

"Greetings, spirit," Wongwang said. "What is it you want of me?"

"Do you know that monk that moved in a little way up the mountain from here?"

"I know he is there, but I have never spoken to him."

"Better that you haven't because he is a very bad person. He practices black magic, and his hermitage blocks the paths I usually like to take around the mountain. He really needs to leave, or I might make something bad happen to him. Can you go and ask him to move somewhere else?"

The next morning, Wongwang went to pay a call on his neighbor. It was the first time Wongwang had left his cave since he moved in, and it felt good to be out in the fresh air and sunshine. It didn't take long for Wongwang to arrive at the other monk's hermitage. He knocked on the door, and the other monk answered.

"What do you want?" the other monk asked.

Wongwang thought him quite rude but said nothing about it.

Instead, he said, "A spirit came to me last night. It said that you have picked a bad place to build your hermitage and that you should leave before a disaster befalls you."

The other monk scoffed. "I'm not going anywhere. You're probably just annoyed to have a neighbor and are making up a story about a spirit to get me to leave. Anyway, my magic is very powerful. Nothing is going to harm me here. Now go away. I have things to do."

Then the other monk slammed his door in Wongwang's face. Wongwang said nothing but turned around and went back to his own hermitage.

That night, the spirit came back to Wongwang's cave.

"Well?" the spirit asked. "Did you talk to that wretched monk who lives over there?"

Wongwang was afraid of the spirit, so said that he had not visited the other monk.

The spirit shook its head. "Foolish monk, I followed you yesterday, and I heard everything that was said. That bad monk will regret not listening to you."

As soon as the spirit was done speaking, it vanished.

In the middle of the night, Wongwang was awakened by a terrible noise. It sounded like the world was ending. Wongwang ran outside of the cave, where he saw that a monstrous landslide had come down the mountain and obliterated both the other monk and his hermitage.

The next day, Wongwang did all his usual things, and in the evening, the spirit came back.

"What do you think of that?" the spirit asked. "Did I scare you?"

"Yes, it was quite startling," Wongwang replied.

"Well, I am three thousand years old, after all. And I'm very good at magic. I also know a lot of important things about the future. For instance, I know that if you continue skulking here in your little cave, you won't do very much good for anyone else, and what's the point of being a holy monk if you never help others? I think you should go to China. You can study the Dharma there and bring that wisdom back to your own people here."

"Oh, indeed, I would love to go to China. I've always wanted to study there. I'm sure I could learn so very much. But I have no idea how to get there."

"Just pay attention, then, and I'll teach you the way."

The monk listened to everything the spirit told him, and in the morning, he packed up his belongings and set out for China. The monk followed the spirit's instructions exactly. He spent eleven years studying Confucianism and the Dharma and much other wisdom besides. At the end of those eleven years, Wongwang returned to Korea as part of a Chinese envoy's entourage. While they were at sea, a dragon came up out of the waves and spoke to Wongwang.

"You are a holy monk," the dragon said.

"Yes, I try to be holy," Wongwang said. "How can I serve you, honorable dragon?"

"When you get home, build a monastery in my honor. And in the monastery, you must teach all the good things you learned while you were in China."

"It shall be done as you ask," Wongwang said, and then the dragon dove back down to the bottom of the sea.

The first thing Wongwang did when he arrived home was to climb Samgi Mountain and go to his old cave because he wanted to thank the spirit who had given him so much good help.

Wongwang had his evening meal and then prepared for sleep, but no sooner had he laid down than the spirit came back.

"So, you're back from China, then," the spirit said. "Did you have a good journey?"

"Oh, yes," Wongwang replied. "It was splendid. I had safe passage both ways, and I learned everything I wanted to know and more. I cannot thank you enough for your help."

"Good. I'm glad it was successful. But you can't stay here too long. I know about your promise to the dragon. You have to get started on that monastery right away."

"Yes, I know I do, but I don't know where to build it."

"I had a chat with the dragon the other day. He thinks that somewhere north of Unmun would be best. Look for the spot where a flock of magpies is gathered. That's the sign that you should build there. I'll come along and help you get started."

In the morning, the monk and the spirit journeyed to the north of Unmun. There they saw a flock of magpies pecking at the ground.

"Here's the spot for the monastery," the spirit said. "Shall we get to work?"

The spirit and the monk worked together to clear the land. Under all the scrub brush, they found a ruined pagoda. They put it back together and set it upright. When the people of the district found out that a wise monk wanted to build a monastery in that place, they came to help build it. Soon a fine monastery dedicated to the sea dragon rose up in the field where the pagoda had been. Wongwang became the abbot, and men and boys came from miles around to join him as his monks and learn what Wongwang had to teach.

Some years after the monastery was established, the spirit appeared to Wongwang one last time.

"I am here to say goodbye," the spirit said. "Although I am a spirit, I am mortal. I am to die soon."

"I am very sad to hear that," Wongwang said. "You have been a good friend to me."

"Is there anything you would ask of me before I go?"

"Yes. May I see what you actually look like?"

"Look to the east at dawn. You will see my arm. That is all I will be able to show you."

Wongwang did as the spirit bid him. In the east, he saw a giant arm rise out of the earth.

Then he heard the spirit's voice say, "I have shown you my arm. Now I will tell you where I must go to die."

The spirit gave Wongwang directions to the place, and the next day, Wongwang went there as the spirit bid him. In that place, a black fox lay on the grass, struggling to breathe. The fox took one last breath and died. Then Wongwang knew that his spirit friend had passed away.

Wongwang went back to his monastery and resumed his teaching. After a time, a dragon began to attend Wongwang's lectures. She found his wisdom worth listening to, and Wongwang liked hearing what she had to say. Now, not long after the dragon began coming to the monastery to hear Wongwang, the country fell into a drought. It hadn't rained for the longest time, and all the crops and herds were suffering. Famine was sure to follow soon if no rain came.

The next time the dragon came to the monastery, Wongwang said, "Honorable Lady Dragon, might I ask a favor of you?"

"Certainly," the dragon replied. "I have enjoyed your teachings very much and will gladly help you in return for all the wisdom I have gained."

"We are having a bad drought, honorable one. Famine is sure to come if we get no rain soon. Can you make it rain for us, please?"

"Oh, no. Rain is in the power of the King of Heaven. If I make it rain for you, the King of Heaven will be angry and will punish me severely."

"Have no fear. If you make it rain and save us from famine, I will protect you."

"Very well," the dragon said, and no sooner had she spoken than a great rainstorm started on the mountainside and worked its way across the country. Suddenly, there was a great clap of thunder.

"Oh, no," the dragon cried. "That was the King of Heaven. He is very angry and will kill me!"

"Hide here," Wongwang said, pointing to a space under the bench where he sat to give his lectures.

The dragon squeezed herself into the space, and when she was settled, Wongwang said, "Now keep still. I'll take care of everything."

The dragon had barely gotten herself as comfortable as she could in that small space when a man strode into the lecture hall.

"I am here on behalf of the King of Heaven," he said. "Where is that disobedient dragon? It is my duty to execute her."

"I'm afraid she heard you coming and turned herself into that pear tree just outside, there," Wongwang replied. "Any punishment you have to mete out needs to be given to the tree."

"Very well," the man said, and then a bolt of lightning struck the tree and clove it in two.

When the man was gone, the dragon crept out of her hiding place and asked what had happened. Wongwang explained about the tree, and in gratitude for taking her punishment for her, the dragon healed the tree and made it whole again.

Wongwang remained at his temple for the rest of his life, giving his wisdom away to any who would listen. He thus fulfilled the spirit's wish: that he uses his wisdom to make the world a better place.

Here's another book by Captivating History that you might like

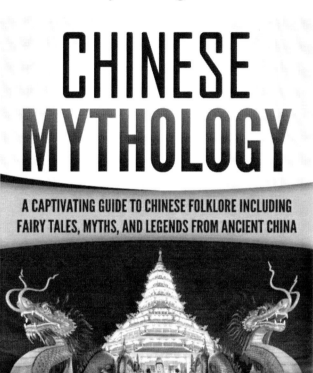

Free Bonus from Captivating History (Available for a Limited time)

Hi History Lovers!

Now you have a chance to join our exclusive history list so you can get your first history ebook for free as well as discounts and a potential to get more history books for free! Simply visit the link below to join.

Captivatinghistory.com/ebook

Also, make sure to follow us on Facebook, Twitter and Youtube by searching for Captivating History.

Bibliography

Korea: Its Land, People, and Culture of All Ages. 2nd ed. Seoul: Hakwon-sa Ltd., 1963.

Allen, H. N. *Korean Tales: Being a Collection of Stories Translated from the Korean Folk Lore.* New York: G. P. Putnam's Sons, 1889.

Carpenter, Frances. *Tales of a Korean Grandmother.* Rutland: Charles E. Tuttle & Company, 1973.

Chung Myung-sub, ed. *Encyclopedia of Korean Folk Beliefs.* Seoul: National Folk Museum of Korea, 2013.

Cotterell, Arthur, ed. *World Mythology.* Bath: Parragon Publishing, 1999.

Grayson, James Huntley. *Myths and Legends from Korea: An Annotated Compendium of Ancient and Modern Materials.* Richmond, Surrey: Curzon Press, 2001.

Griffis, William Elliot. *Korean Fairy Tales.* New York: Thomas Y. Crowell Company, 1911.

———. *The Unmannerly Tiger and Other Korean Tales.* New York: Thomas Y. Crowell Company, 1911.

Holstein, John. *The Magpie Bridge.* Seoul: Si-sa-yong-o-sa Inc., 1985.

Hwang, Pae-gang. *Korean Myths and Folk Legends.* Trans. Young-Hie Han, Se-Joong Kim, and Seung-Pyong Hwae. Fremont: Jain Publishing Company, 2006.

Kim, Kichung. *An Introduction to Classical Korean Literature: From Hyangga to P'ansori.* n.c.: Routledge, n.d. Accessed on Google Books 22 March 2021. <http://www.google.com/books>

Kwon, Holly H. *The Moles and the Mireuk: A Korean Folktale.* Boston: Houghton Mifflin Company, 1993.

Lee, Clare, Isaac Durst, and Keirin Lee. *Gyonu and Jingnyo.* [publication information is in Korean and therefore inaccessible to this author]

Lee, Peter H., ed. *Sourcebook of Korean Civilization.* Vol. 1: *From Early Times to the Sixteenth Century.* New York: Columbia University Press, 1993.

———. *Anthology of Korean Literature: From Early Times to the Nineteenth Century.* Honolulu: The University Press of Hawaii, 1981.

———. *Anthology of Korean Poetry from the Earliest Era to the Present.* New York: The John Day Company, 1964.

McCann, David R. *Early Korean Literature: Selections and Introductions.* New York: Columbia University Press, 2000.

Park, Janie Jaehyun. *The Love of Two Stars: A Korean Legend.* Toronto: House of Anansi Press, 2005.

Verniero, Joan C. *One-Hundred-and-One-Asian Read-Aloud Myths and Legends.* New York: Black Dog & Leventhal Publishers, 2001.

Voorhees, Duance, and Mark Mueller. *The Woodcutter and the Heavenly Maidens, The Firedogs.* Rev. ed. Elizabeth, Hollym Corporation, 2008.

———. *The Faithful Daughter, Shim Ch'ong.* Elizabeth: Hollym Corporation, 1990.

Printed by BoD™ in Norderstedt, Germany